to eternity

LESSONS We've LEARNED on
Dating and Marriage

Al & Ben
CARRAWAY

CFI, an Imprint of Cedar Fort, Inc.
Springville, Utah

ISBN 13: 978-1-4621-2091-8

Published by CFI, an imprint of Cedar Fort, Inc.
2373 W. 700 S., Springville, UT 84663
Distributed by Cedar Fort, Inc., www.cedarfort.com

LIBRARY OF CONGRESS CATALOGING-IN-PUBLICATION DATA

Names: Carraway, Al, 1988- author. | Carraway, Ben, 1991- author.
Title: Cheers to eternity : what we've learned on dating and marriage / Al
   Carraway and Ben Carraway.
Description: Springville, UT : Published by CFI, an imprint of Cedar Fort,
   Inc., [2017] | Includes bibliographical references and index.
Identifiers: LCCN 2017022975 (print) | LCCN 2017027192 (ebook) | ISBN
   9781462128310 (ebook) | ISBN 9781462120918 (pbk. : alk. paper)
Subjects: LCSH: Marriage--Religious aspects--Church of Jesus Christ of
   Latter-day Saints. | Marriage--Religious aspects--Mormon Church. | Marital
   dating. | Church of Jesus Christ of Latter-day Saints--Doctrines. | Mormon
   Church--Doctrines.
Classification: LCC BX8643.M36 (ebook) | LCC BX8643.M36 C37 2017 (print) |
   DDC 248.8/44--dc23
LC record available at https://lccn.loc.gov/2017022975

Cover design by Shawnda T. Craig
Cover design © 2017 by Cedar Fort, Inc.
Edited by Hali Bird, Chelsea Holdaway, and Kaitlin Barwick
Typeset by Chelsea Holdaway

Printed in the United States of America

10 9 8 7 6 5 4 3 2 1

Printed on acid-free paper

Cheers

to eternity

Dedicated to

Gracie + Christian

PRAISE FOR
CHEERS TO ETERNITY

"These inspiring words are filled with so many positive vibes; Al and Ben make you feel that any relationship can be peaches and cream. They kind of make me want to get married again . . . uhh, you know what I mean."

—Jon Heder, actor from *Blades of Glory*, *Napoleon Dynamite*, and *Pickle and Peanut*

"*Cheers to Eternity* is a stellar book for anyone in a relationship. The book is funny, thoughtful, informative, and very real. Al and Ben use amazing experiences from their life and others' lives that are relatable to everyone. I love how they remind us all to laugh every day and to try and not take everything so seriously all the time. They have an awesome perspective on dating, marriage, and life in general. Loved reading this book!"

— Jimmer Fredette, professional basketball player

"I first met Al and Ben when they were engaged, so I have been blessed to watch their marriage and family develop from the beginning. I'm proud of them for all they have learned and for their willingness to now teach the rest of us with their trademark honesty and candor. This book will validate the good things you are doing and remind you of a few things you can do better. Most of all, it will reassure you that with God all things are possible—especially a strong and happy marriage."

—Brad Wilcox, BYU professor and author of *The Continuous Atonement* and *Changed through His Grace*

"When Nephi built a ship, it was said to have been made 'not after the manner of men.' It reminds me of this book. It is very unique, and you can tell from page one that this book was God-inspired! This book is an absolute home run, and I guarantee you that by the time you've finished the book, you'll be begging for a sequel!"

—Alex Boyé, award-winning singer, songwriter, and YouTuber

"Al and Ben hit a home run with this book. If you're married or hoping to be married one day, their message is for you. I felt like I was having a fun conversation with old friends. Each chapter is authentic and relevant. And while they don't skip the tough issues, I found myself laughing out loud at their funny back-and-forth style. Don't put this book back on the shelf; it's worth your time."

—Hank Smith, PhD, author of *Be Happy*

"It's so easy to get carried away with the Carraways! Ben and Al's conversation-style book on marriage will make you laugh, cry, and feel all the feels. Their candor is refreshing and their chemistry as a couple comes to life on each page. Filled with lessons they've learned thus far on their journey together, their book speaks openly and easily about not just the ups but also the downs that accompany even the best marriages. Whether you're just thinking about marriage or you've been in the matrimony game for quite some time, Ben and Al's insights will speak to you. Their words of truth remind us that if Jesus can turn water into wine, then He can make a Christ-centered marriage truly divine—so *cheers to eternity*!"

—Zandra Vranes, speaker and author of *Diary of Two Mad Black Mormons*

Also by Al Carraway

More than the Tattooed Mormon

I Know journal

Set Goals. Say Prayers. Work Hard. journal

With God, Life Is Oh So Good journal

CONTENTS

Contents

ACKNOWLEDGMENTS

To Facebook for helping us to meet each other virtually online. When we lived across the country from one another, it was you that was our source of communication. Without Facebook messenger, we're not sure where we would be.

To the hit TV show *The Office* for the laughter and joy you bring us. (But not to the screen on Netflix that pops up asking us, "Are you still watching *The Office*?" Yes, Netflix, we are. And now you've ruined another cuddle sesh because you're making us get up and look for the remote to hit "continuing playing.")

To Benjamin's 1993 Toyota Camry. We miss you. Rest in peace. In the summer of 2013, you logged over 5,000 miles for Al to speak all over Utah, Nevada, Wyoming, and Idaho. You sacrificed your engine for our relationship to flourish.

To New York and Arizona for being the greatest states with the greatest food.

Acknowledgments

To our children, Gracie and Christian. We love and adore you. You are both bright lights to us and those around you. You have made us better people and our lives profoundly sweeter. You have helped us understand God in ways we couldn't have learned without you.

To all our parents, family members, relatives, and friends who have supported us in our lives. You have shaped us into who we are now. Thank you!

PREFACE

INTRODUCTION

If you want something to last forever, you treat it differently. You shield it and protect it. You never abuse it. You don't expose it to the elements. You don't make it common or ordinary. If it ever becomes tarnished, you lovingly polish it until it gleams like new. It becomes special because you have made it so, and it grows more beautiful and precious as time goes by.
—Elder F. Burton Howard[1]

Marriage is the holiest and highest ordinance, binding man and woman together throughout the eternities. So let's make sure we are doing what we can to build up and work toward a happy and healthy marriage! We are by no means claiming to have all the answers—and the last thing we want to do is come off as self-righteous—but one credential we do have (if we can call it that) is that we *love* being married. And we work on improving our marriage all the time. This book is a compilation of experiences, lessons, and counsel we have learned from our single lives up to this exact moment, typing this at our kitchen table and listening to this one awful song that somehow keeps coming up on our Spotify music playlist. This is a compilation of the funny, the hard, and the embarrassing: the things that have all turned into truths and make what we personally have fun, functional, and amazing. We crack jokes, we open up, and we are transparent. We know that no two marriages are the same. Our goal is to be genuine and just keep it real. We hope that what we have learned can help you (whether you're single or newlywed) really make the most out of this life!

Background to Al

I was born and raised in Rochester, New York, where the food is amazing everywhere you go and the culture is diverse and exciting. We are a close-knit family and we always had something to celebrate. Even the littlest of things were celebrated. I'm talking, the whole house is decorated and a big meal is cooked. Our family gatherings with my aunt and cousins were frequent and always very loud. As a family, no matter what we were doing together, it was always a party. The smallest and simplest things were exciting.

I am the baby of three girls, and I was most definitely the rascal of the family. I am independent and self-driven.

My parents separated when I was young, but that never affected how they acted toward my two sisters and me. My dad worked at Kodak most of his life but is most known for being an artist. He paints and he is awesome at it. Most of his stuff is scattered throughout our city in bars and coffee shops. Even though we didn't live with my dad, we saw him all the time. When I was older and lived on my own, I would walk to his house every day and tell him everything.

My mom is the one who primarily raised us. We lived with her, and she did everything you could think of for us. At one point, she worked three jobs because she wanted to give us everything she could. She is one hardworking woman! She always pushed us to be better and to discover more of ourselves and was actively involved in whatever we showed interest in. Growing up, life definitely had the usual bumps in it, but it was still great. If I had a chance to change anything in my life, I wouldn't.

My family and culture taught me to work hard and just make things happen. At age twenty, I honestly thought I had my whole life figured out. I had big goals, the drive to accomplish all of them, and the stubbornness to do it all alone.

I moved out and lived on my own when I was seventeen years old. I graduated college with my degree in graphic design and marketing. And the moment I thought I had my life figured out and everything was going smoothly, I met two boys in suits and doofy helmets riding bikes. Mormon missionaries! I never heard of them before in my life. (When I thought of people in suits preaching the gospel door-to-door I thought of Jehovah's Witnesses). I wasn't interested in religion, I wasn't interested in learning more about God, and I most definitely wasn't interested in changing anything in my life. I thought religion was something people turned to when something was going wrong in their life, as some sort of mental comfort, and that wasn't me. I was happy—as happy as I thought I could be in life.

I humored them and I listened because I felt bad, and because they were so precious looking. My motives were definitely skewed at first. I just wanted to prove to them they didn't need to live a certain way to be happy, and that all of these blessings they were working toward weren't real; they were all in their head. Long story short, joke's on me, because the funny thing about living the commandments, trying to improve, and turning to God is that you're blessed. I changed unconsciously. Better opportunities started coming up. I was happier; I was stronger; I was guided. Even though I didn't want the gospel to be true, the reality is God is real. He speaks to us. He helps us become better, and He leads us to the *best* things.

I'll leave my conversion to The Church of Jesus Christ of Latter-day Saints to my first book *More Than the Tattooed Mormon* (shameless plug, no big deal). Maybe this part of my story isn't too relevant to *this* book, but I do want to preface myself a little bit so you know where I was coming from. Family and friends had left me because of my decision to join the Church. After my baptism, it seemed life had fallen apart, and it didn't seem to get better for a while.

I yelled at God *a lot*. I suffered and felt alone a lot—something that was completely new to me. I forced myself to use the faith I didn't know I had a lot. I cried a lot. But I tried a lot too. I turned to God even more. It took a long time of suffering to finally decide I was tired of it. I was tired of feeling weak, of becoming bitter toward people and my situation, and of not feeling like myself. So, I changed my perspective. I learned that we find what we look for, so we should look for the good. I decided to worry about me and worry about God. And I decided, with every bit of me, to trust the fact that everything is meant to help us succeed. Opportunities, lessons, blessings, and comforts are found every day. Going full steam ahead, I decided to always look for the good; always look for the blessings; and always look for the lessons, opportunities, and strengths. I decided to choose to keep going, to choose faith, and to choose not to get offended or let rude comments or a mean member of the Church come between me and my eternal salvation. Hard times will always be there, but so will Christ. And with Him, we overcome and conquer the world. And to me, that is the greatest reason to be happy every day.

Every question you may have about me and every detail you can imagine is in my other book. I wouldn't be mad if you read it! But I made the difficult decision to leave my family and New York against my will, following a prompting to move across the country. I didn't want to move there but after finding out that God was real, who was I to tell Him He was wrong? So here I was in Utah, trying to live with this new mind-set of having faith to overcome the challenges that came from my move and my decision to follow God. I started writing on my site, alcarraway.com, about my trials and lessons as soon as I got here. I decided to share the helps and lessons I had learned along the way that made even the trials of life enjoyable and rich with meaning. My site grew far greater than anything I could have ever planned or hoped for; my most popular post got over a million views in half a day! Since 2011, I have travelled all over the country, speaking and doing firesides—talking about how to keep going during hard times and the reality of God and this gospel—and have won multiple awards for it. I've even spoken a few times with General Authorities. I've worked at the Church headquarters in social marketing and am still there now. I'm a taco enthusiast and a journal addict, and I am the happiest when doing anything outdoors—or watching *The Office*. I'm most definitely an optimist and a lover of all things good. And I *love* God. I embrace the hard things and am forever grateful that things never went the way I had in mind, because with God, they have been profoundly better.

In relation to this book about dating and marriage, I want to give a shout-out to those who may be losing hope in finding a spouse. I've been there. I can relate and I am sending hope and prayers your way! I definitely got married later than I wanted and later than "the norm." I went through the process of creating a mental list of all the things that were wrong with me because my marriage hadn't happened yet. I wasn't skinny enough; I wasn't a good enough homemaker because I didn't know how to cook or sew; I didn't look temple worthy because of my tattoos, etc.

Then I went through the process of convincing myself that I would just have to settle because maybe this was all my fault and I was expecting too much in a future companion.

It's hard to not take it personally, and it's hard not to lose hope. Especially when it is a righteous, good thing that we're trying to attain—marriage.

But here's me sending that love to you! I'm grateful that I was patient enough to wait to meet my husband, and I'm grateful that I didn't settle or compromise. I truly believe that what I have now with Ben is what I need, and I hate to think about what I would have missed out on or struggled with if I didn't trust God's time frame.

You will be blessed with a companion that will help you in the ways that you need, even if you sometimes feel like they don't exist, or that you're asking for too much, or that you're too picky. Don't let passing time allow doubts or the idea of settling to take over. Just hold on and don't lose confidence. Heavenly Father knows what's important to us and He knows what we need; He will bless us with those things if we trust Him and stay close to Him.

In the meantime, go on adventures and learn new hobbies. Don't put your life on pause. Fill your life with meaning and purpose, and stop thinking that there is something wrong with you. Just be you and take care of the relationship you do have: your relationship with God.

Background to Benjamin

Ich bin geboren in der schönen Stadt Nürnberg Deutschland. English: I was born in the beautiful city of Nürnberg, Germany. I'm in no way fluent in German (yet), but I am learning it. I lived in Germany for the first couple years of my life. My dad, who has served in both the Marines and the US Army, was serving in the US military and was stationed there. My Grandfather Cross fought and served in World War II, and my Grandfather Carraway served in Vietnam. My family moved from Germany to Utah when I was just over two years old. My parents are converts and moved to Utah on faith and prayers alone. There was no family, no job, no car, and no home for them in Utah. We lived in the basement of a friend from Germany. The move to Utah wasn't always easy for my family, but my parents knew that God told them to move there and that it was right. And so, my family ended up in the Salt Lake Valley.

I was a very active boy, always outside getting into trouble and playing sports, mostly basketball and football. While I don't play either sport anymore, they have been a big part of my life. Instead, I just enjoy watching sports whenever I have the free time. As I am getting older, I have also developed a love for education. I just can't seem to learn enough. I'm big on self-development; it's a passion in my life. I am always trying to look for ways to improve and help others to do the same.

I was raised in West Valley City, Utah. I grew up in somewhat humble circumstances. We never had much money, but my parents always did the best they could to give my siblings and me everything we needed. We always seemed to make everything work out. My parents are wonderful. They always showed us love and gave us all the attention we needed. I lived in a home where faith was always taught. My parents are converts to the LDS Church. Shortly after their marriage, they met the LDS missionaries in North Carolina, when my dad was stationed there with the Marines. My parents take their faith seriously because of the impact it has had on their life. I grew up participating in every way at church. I was responsible for giving my Primary and Sunday School teachers a lot of gray hair (if you're reading this, please forgive me). I was very active in Boy Scouts, and I am an Eagle Scout. Even though I grew up in a solidly faithful family, I never took the gospel seriously. I took it for granted. I didn't think it was for me. I have always believed in Heavenly Father and in Jesus Christ, but I just didn't think the gospel or the LDS Church was something I wanted to be a part of. When I was a teen in high school, I kind of drifted away from the Church. I got into things I shouldn't have, made poor decisions, and created bad habits. I was off track and living far below my potential.

When I was eighteen, my entire life changed! My eyes were opened because of my circumstances. I was compelled to be humble when my life came crashing down. At eighteen years old, I thought I had it made. I had many friends and a very active social life, and I had accepted a track-and-field scholarship to a school in Oklahoma. I ran the four hundred meters and jumped in the long jump. They say that white men can't jump, and that's true for about 98 percent of us! But not me. I had hops! I was excited for this scholarship. But shortly after graduation, I received an email letting me know that my scholarship was no longer offered. I was devastated. To this day, I don't know why it was taken away.

After losing my scholarship, I started to lose everything. I lost all but a few of my friends left and right after graduation, and girls I was dating suddenly seemed uninterested. What was even more devastating was when the housing market crashed during the huge financial crisis of 2007–2008 and my parents lost their home. The home I grew up in was now gone. All of that impacted me. A big part of who I am today I credit to the things I lost and experienced when I was eighteen years old. Thankfully, we were blessed to find a place in South Jordan, Utah, to call home. In that home in South Jordan, my life would change forever.

The first couple of months living in that home, I was depressed and living in a pretty dark state. I felt alone. I felt broken. I felt like my life was in pieces. I felt like I had lost everything. The darkness I felt I was in and the fogginess I felt all the time made me question, "Why am I even here? What's the point? What do I do now?" Because of how I was feeling, I started to want to discover why I was feeling this way, which led me to change—or, in Christian terms, to repent.

My conversion/change story is a long story, so I won't include it all. But when I got my answer that I needed to change my life and change what I was doing, I found myself in my bishop's office. He didn't even know who I was; we had never met before. I felt like I was about to blow his mind when I confessed everything. I was nervous. I almost chickened out. That bishop changed my life. He was so accepting, and he embraced me. He didn't care about my screwups or shortcomings. He helped me get on the path to receive forgiveness. Every month, we would meet, and through his help, I really felt like I received forgiveness.

No one told me I had to change just because I was at the right age to go on a mission. Growing up, I didn't want to serve an LDS mission. I never wanted to. I would argue with my dad over mission talk. No missionary has ever served in my family's history. I didn't know what a mission was, and I thought you just knocked on doors every day, all day for two years. Who wants to do that? But when you change, you naturally seem to have a desire to help others. So, with prayer, God told me to serve a mission. I decided to serve, and that decision will forever bless my life. I served in the Pennsylvania Philadelphia Mission, English- and Ebonics-speaking. Everything I have today is because of that decision. I would have never met Al if I didn't go on a mission. If I never lost my track scholarship or my friends, if this girl I liked never broke things off with me, and if my parents never lost their home, I never would have changed. I like to credit losing everything I had before to gaining everything I have now. Heavenly Father loved me enough that He was willing to hurt me by having me lose things, so that I could wake up and get on the right path.

My life hasn't always been easy. I've made plenty of mistakes, but who hasn't? Things haven't gone as planned, but I have no regrets. Zero. I wouldn't change anything. I firmly believe I was destined to have this life and journey through it. Even my foolish mistakes were part of my journey. It's through those exact things that I truly came to *know* and love God, and I truly learned how to turn to Him and rely and trust Him and His will.

Two quotes I really admire,

> If you're not making mistakes, then you're not doing anything. I'm positive that a doer makes mistakes.
> –John Wooden[2]

> We are here to make mistakes.
> –a five-year-old boy from northeastern
> Pennsylvania told me that piece of wisdom

Mistakes or sins are going to happen. When they do, get over it. It's a part of our life here on earth. It's what we do after we stumble that truly matters. Did we change? Did we fix what needed fixing? If yes, then move on! Because God already has.

There have been many leaders and individuals that have influenced my life for good and have helped me discover my true potential. My goal is to help others discover their true potential. I would not be who I am today without these certain individuals. Their influence has helped shape me into the man, husband, and father

I am today. They helped me discover who I am. So, thank you to my wife, Al, and to Mom and Dad. Also a big thank you to Craig H., Josh R., Jody C., Mike C., Curt D., Bill S., Chris R., Luis D., Rebecca S., David W., David J., Trent B., Adam P., and Sam B. You da real MVP!

CONVERSATIONS

How We Met

Ben: Al and I met under unusual circumstances. I was serving my mission in Philadelphia, Pennsylvania, and my mission was one of five or seven missions piloting Facebook missionary work for the Church. I had been out on my mission for about eight months or so when I was contacting some investigators on Facebook and came across a video titled "Dear Elder" that Al had made. As I watched it, I remember thinking, *Wow, this girl has a really cool story.* The words of the video definitely touched me because I was going through a tough time on my mission. So I posted her video on my Facebook, and when I did that, Al pretty much became known in my mission with the missionaries. After that, pretty much my whole mission added her as a friend. One day, she added me on Facebook.

Al: *He added me,* for the record.

Ben: I had no intentions of talking to her at all, and we barely spoke for a while.

Al: We talked so sparingly; we first started out just talking about the Church and the people he was teaching.

Ben: I messaged her one day about her story because she is from New York and was from the same demographic as some of the people I was teaching at that time. I thought her story could help some of them and help my companion and me find ways to help them.

She sent me a message on Facebook to wish me a happy birthday, and that was the first time we had said something that wasn't gospel related. I said "Thanks," and she just kept asking me all these questions! Like, "When do you come home?" "Where do you live?" and la-la-la. She was saying that when I got home we should hang out and go to the temple.

Al: Wait, no, hold on. I wasn't like, right off the bat, "Let's go to the temple." I'm not that weird or creepy!

Ben: No, that was the first day, I still remember.

Al: The first day? Are you real-life right now? 'Cause I'm pretty sure it was like a week before you came home from your mission that I found out that you lived thirty minutes away from me, and you had never been to the Salt Lake Temple.

Ben: No, babe, it was the very first day. You said, "When you get home, we should hang out and go to the temple."

Al: I don't know if I believe this story.

Ben: I do. But we'd hardly ever talked to each other, and we didn't know each other at all. And here she was, asking me all these kinds of questions about home. I still had eight to nine months left on my mission and home was never something I wanted to think about, because it would distract me and it was just really weird. I went to sign off of Facebook and she said, "Well, you'd better talk to me tomorrow when you get on." So I did.

Al: He was allowed online every day for an hour, and I would always look forward to when he would sign on, mostly because I had a desk job and was bored. I was online all day while I was at work, so it's not like I went out of my way for it. I wasn't expecting anything to come out of talking to him; I just did it because I enjoyed talking to him about the Church and hearing about his mission. I liked hearing about who he was teaching and things they were struggling with because, as a convert, it was all so familiar to me. I never wrote him any letters or sent him packages. We did, however, toward the end of his mission, make and send video messages to each other. I think at that point, we knew so much about each other that we wanted to see each other's mannerisms and personalities come through. So that's what we did, and we ended up just sending videos to each other for the rest of his mission.

Ben: We would only send videos to each other about once a month, and our videos became our form of writing letters to each other. When summer ended, I was honestly surprised that we were still talking. Of course I was interested in her and getting to know her more, and when I came home, sure, I would love to have her be single and take her on a date. But my thoughts were that I still had six months left in my mission. I thought she would get tired of talking to me or our conversations would die out, and because she's beautiful as all get-out I thought for sure she would be snatched up and wife'd up. I mean, she *was* living in Provo.

Al: I was so excited when he had three months left because we had become such good friends. Through all of this, I was still going on dates, so who knows what could've happened. I remember he made a video and it said, "Just a few weeks left!" Reality hit and I thought, *Holy shoot! Now I* have *to hang out with him.* I mean, we wrote to each other for this long; it would be silly not to meet in person, but I was terrified. I never thought it would actually last this long, and now that it had, I was worried we'd meet and I wouldn't have that connection and I wouldn't see him again. Or maybe he wanted more than a friendship, and I didn't feel the same way. I was worried all that time we spent talking to each other would have been wasted and our friendship would be ruined.

Ben: Toward the end of my mission, the writing became more consistent. I was going home in a few weeks, reality started to set in, and I knew home was coming. My last two transfers were *busy*; I saw a lot of success. All the while, I was still talking to Al and I thought, *Wow, this may actually happen.* I would say prayers that Al would be off of my mind during the day so I could just focus on missionary work, and that she'd stay single. I prayed just asking if this was something to pursue.

Al: I didn't know that. That's so cute!

Ben: When I got off my mission, right after being released, I went in my room to give her a call. I was pacing my floor and it took me a little bit of time to press send because I was nervous to call; it was so weird that I wasn't a missionary anymore and I was going to call a girl. I called, and without even saying "hi," I just said, "Do you know who this is?" She was really excited and that broke the tension. We decided to hang out a few days later. The next thing I know, she sends me a text saying, "Good night, handsome."

Al: I did not!

Ben: Yes, you did, no lie! So I immediately thought, *Man, this girl wants me bad.* And you couldn't resist!

Al: That's ridiculous; who let him tell the story here? This is an inaccurate portrayal of how we met.

Ben: We made plans to hang out a day later. We decided to go do a session in the Salt Lake Temple and go get steaks afterward for dinner. I've never been to a live endowment session before, and she wanted to take me to one, so that's what we did.

Al: I feel like going to the temple on your first date is a terrible idea. How weird is that, right? But in my mind, I wasn't thinking that this was a serious date or anything. I thought we were just going to hang out. I was endowed, and Fridays were my temple day! I wasn't going to miss that, even if I was meeting someone.

Ben: My car was still being worked on in my garage, so Al had to come pick me up. When I heard the doorbell ring, I was so nervous.

Al: I saw him peek through the blinds of his front window, and then he didn't answer the door. I was standing there for a few minutes, in the middle of winter, on his front porch.

Ben: I was too nervous to open the door, so I took a deep breath and thought, *I hope she likes me. All I have to*

*do is be myself because if she is really going to like me she
is going to like me for who I am.*

Al: When he did finally open the door, my very first
thought was, *Uh-oh! I'm in trouble.* In a good way!
I went on enough dates with enough guys to know
that as soon as I saw him, something was different
than every other date I'd been on. It was like a heart-
stopping kind of "uh-oh."

Ben: When I saw her, I was just blown away and thought,
Stab me in the heart with those eyes! I was just struck
with how beautiful she was. So we left to go to the
Salt Lake Temple. On the way there, everything just
felt natural and it wasn't awkward at all; we were listening to music, laughing, and just having a good
time together.

Al: Yeah, it wasn't weird at all. It was like we'd been out
a million times before; we talked and laughed the
entire time. After the session, when we were sitting
together in the celestial room, Ben did one of those
fake yawns and put his arm around me.

Ben: I didn't yawn and put my around you, I just put
my arm around you! Anyway, she just kept snug-
gling closer and closer to me and put her head on my
shoulder. Then Al looked me in the eyes and said,
"We need to get married."

Al: So, none of that actually happened. Ben just likes to spice up the story a little. The fake yawn I'm pretty sure did happen, though. We went to go get steak, and he was such an open book that night: telling me his story, where he came from, his life's passions and goals. I was actually getting freaked out because he was touching on all of those spiritual needs that I wanted and it was scary!

Ben: I just wanted to be myself right from the start and have her know the real me. I remember feeling that night that I was spiritually attracted to her. The feeling was so strong, and I had never felt that attraction with anyone before. It was definitely one of the strongest feelings I have ever felt.

Al: Yeah, I had that same feeling and it was scary because we still hadn't really hung out and still didn't really know each other. So anyway, we left dinner and he said, "Let's go for a drive to the Draper Temple and look at the view to see all the city lights."

Ben: I didn't want the night to end.

Al: We sat in the car talking and listening to Coldplay's song "Green Eyes." You know how when you are about to be kissed, you're like an inch away from each other's face, and they have that look in their eyes? That happened. So, even though I am *pro* at playing hard to get and absolutely never ever kiss on the first date, I liked him enough to not leave him hanging or embarrass him. So as he leaned in for the 90 percent, I went in the 10 percent to kiss him back. He purposely didn't end up kissing me. He gave me an Eskimo kiss instead, and I was totally embarrassed.

Ben: I thought it was funny. She blushed, and that's when I leaned in and gave her probably the best kiss she'd ever had.

Al: Oh, brother . . .

Ben: Well, sparks did fly, and she drove me home. I hated to see her leave. All I could think about that night and the rest of that weekend was her, and how I wanted to see her again. I prayed that morning about her, asking that I would know what I should do next. I didn't want to rush into anything if it wasn't what God wanted.

Dating

Ben: I had my homecoming talk two days after our first date, and out of all the people that came, I was most excited to see Al again.

Al: After his homecoming talk, I went to his house and he showed me all of his mission photos, even though I had already seen most of them, and then we went on a really long walk. At the end of the walk, he asked me to be his girlfriend! I was so shocked because this was only the second time we had hung out, and I told him no! I told him that he needed to date other girls first to figure out what he wanted. He didn't go for that.

Ben: I had dated enough before my mission to know what I wanted. I understood what she meant by that, but I liked her so much already, I didn't need to date around because Al had what I was looking for. I wanted Al and I wasn't going to miss out on her.

Al: So even though I was terrified and thought that this was crazy, we started dating.

Ben: I actually thought she would text me that night and tell me she had changed her mind and that we were moving too fast.

Al: I was thinking about doing that, but I prayed about it first and felt calm about it all. As soon as we started dating, we would go to the temple weekly and sometimes twice a week together. We did that because (1) we loved the temple and I made sure that I kept up with my habit of going every week; I wasn't going to let anyone or anything stop me from doing that; and (2) we wanted to make sure we started our relationship off spiritually.

I think it was during our second full week of dating that I was on the cover of the *LDS Living* magazine, which caused my speaking engagements to blow up! It was summertime, and we spent most of our dating time in the car driving to my firesides, spending *at least* four hours a night in the car. During those car rides, we would talk about anything and everything. We were so open with each other right off the bat, and we told each other everything. We got to know almost everything about each other very quickly.

Ben: We never went to the movies or did any other activities because her schedule was so crazy that we didn't have time to do "typical" dates. Our dating relationship was spent in the car, talking and making up games, and it was a blast! We joke and say we had a car courtship, and we really did.

Al: If you really want to get to know someone, go on a really long road trip with them; you will see what kind of person they are. During those times of getting to know Ben, I was afraid that my life, and who I used to be, would be an issue like it had been in the past. I was seriously convinced that I would never get married. I got along with everyone that I went on dates with, and I think most of them liked the idea of me. But when it came down to it, it bothered them that I didn't come from a strong LDS family and that I didn't look temple worthy. I saw other girls getting asked out on dates and couldn't help but notice that I wasn't like them. I didn't know how to sew my own skirts, I couldn't play piano, and (other than pasta) cooking was just a no-go. Although I was confidant in who I was, after years of being single and living in Utah, I thought that I was forever going to be overlooked. But those things didn't bother Ben, and he fully accepted me for who I was.

Ben: What mattered to me was not someone's past, but where they were now and where they wanted to go. I loved her for who she was and what she was doing. Her life before the Church didn't bother me at all. Truthfully, I felt like I wanted someone who had a story of her own, because I too had my own past. But what I really needed was someone who was passionate about the gospel. Al accepted that, and I had always wanted someone who could understand me on all levels.

Al: I remember one time we went and did sealings only a few weeks into us dating, and *during* the ordinance, the sealer stopped and asked Ben, "So when's the date?" Ben turned so red! It was so funny and awkward because we hadn't brought up marriage to each other yet. Ben mumbled even more awkwardly that we didn't have a date. Then the sealer totally called him out. He said that he "shouldn't wait with this one," and that we should get married to each other. Then he started the ordinance over again and moved on.

Ben: That sealer sparked it in my mind to start thinking about marrying Al. So I did. I started to pray about it, felt awesome about it, and I brought it up to her one night at Ensign Peak.

Al: When he brought up marriage, I was so shocked and taken aback because we had been only dating for *a month*. I was so scared that I didn't talk to him for the whole rest of the night. Awkward, right? That was a long drive home.

Ben: I thought I made you so upset. She shut me down, and we had a long, awkward, quiet drive back to Provo. You can imagine my anxiety and the thoughts that were running through my head: *Did I blow it? Was it too soon?*

Al: I told him we couldn't get married because he hadn't even seen me mad yet! How am I supposed to marry someone when he hasn't seen me mad and heard me yell? But, what do you know, a few days later, I came around. We pursued getting married and even went out one night looking for rings. That, my friends, is a product of prayer and the Spirit. Doing crazy things that don't make sense, but that you feel you should do anyway.

Ben: For Al it was too soon, but she got over it. I mean, she couldn't resist me; she just liked me too much. A few days later, we went ring shopping for me to get some ideas. How I knew that Al was the one I should marry was quite easy. I mean, I loved being with her all day long and would never get tired of it. But I really felt it on our very first date. It was mostly a spiritual attraction. Every time I was with her, I had a strong pull toward her. Being around her just made me want to be an even better person. She was (and still is) always seeking ways to be closer to God. She didn't let anything come between her and her relationship with Him, her spiritual habits, or the goals she had for her future and her day-to-day living. I did a lot of talking to God to see if it was in His cards for us to get married, and I felt so good about it that I knew the answer was that this was right.

Al: For me, it wasn't a huge overwhelming answer that marrying him was right. It was a subtle calm that brought excitement. When I thought about marrying him, I didn't have any bad feelings about it. Of course, with a big decision like marriage, fear will slip into your mind. If it was right, I knew that fear would go away and that comfort would come when I was seeking God and the Spirit. If it wasn't right, I figured that the fear wouldn't go away. But it always did. Knowing that marrying him was right all came down to prayer.

Ben: I did have one freak-out moment where I almost called the whole thing off. It was right after I put a deposit down on Al's ring, actually. But it was all for silly, selfish reasons. The following week, Al wrote her popular, hit blog post titled "The Tattooed Mormon," which got over a million views in just one day! She went from dozens of people who knew her, to everyone knowing her and wanting her to come speak at a fireside. She went from one or two speaking engagements a week, to literally one every day, sometimes twice a day. It was nuts. The same weekend that blog post was released, we went to general conference together and almost never made it home due to line of people wanting to take their picture with her. I was off to the side by myself for two hours; I wasn't happy at all.

Al: We had our first argument that day. I'm glad we got that out of the way before we got married!

Ben: I didn't like having to compete for time with her; I didn't like going out in public and being stopped and having to take a picture. I didn't like waitresses not leaving us alone while we were out on a date. It was tough. I remember thinking, *Well, I just put a couple hundred dollars down on a deposit for the ring; is this what I really wanted? Was I as committed as I thought I was? Should I go through with this?*

I had a few friends and people I know tease me about dating someone "famous" and "popular." I received emails and Facebook messages from people saying that I didn't deserve her, or telling me how I should break up with her because of her hectic schedule. It was tough reading those emails and messages, not just from people I knew but even from people I didn't. I let those stupid, but mainly selfish, thoughts come into my head, and that was affecting my relationship with her. I remember letting her take my car to a fireside in the Salt Lake area and as I saw her drive away, I sat outside on the deck, praying and pondering. I remember feeling, *Ben, you have two choices, (1) forget all about yourself and focus on her. Love her, support her and no matter what, be there for her, or (2) let her go, and you'll regret the day that you did.* It was like the Spirit smacked me in the face! I knew what I had to do, and I felt sure about what I wanted to do. I wanted her and everything that came with it—fully and completely—and deciding that changed everything. I made that decision to put her first, love her, support her, be there for her, and be happy when she has success. I never looked back and there was a huge difference. I went to every single fireside that she had that summer, except when she flew—that would have been way too pricey.

Al: We traveled all over! Nevada twice, Idaho three times, Las Vegas, and just about every city in Utah. We went to Heber City about six days a week, all within the first few months of knowing each other. We put at least six thousand miles on his car just that summer.

Ben: I loved it; it was so much fun. We made so many amazing memories, and to this day, I miss those busy

34

summer nights traveling all over to new places. I miss those hours we'd spend in the car together every night just talking and laughing. I loved hearing her speak, and seeing the people she's touched. I loved meeting so many new people with her, and those things that initially bothered me are now great joys to me. Making the decision to fully accept and support her, allowed me to have innumerable experiences I will never forget that I wouldn't have ever had unless I had made that decision. When the Spirit told me that day, "Forget yourself, Ben," it made all the difference. It's easy to want to change people or to be selfish, but with love, it should be understanding and selfless. I hope, and it's my goal, to always put Al first and to support her on anything.

There has to be a time where we all make that decision to fully and completely commit to another person. We cannot expect to change the things we do not like about them or their life for our own selfish desires. We need to commit to who they are and their life and everything that comes with that. There will be things that do need to change and that you will need to work on before and after you're married, but ultimately that decision of acceptance will be needed in order to move forward successfully and avoid any unnecessary pitfalls or arguments in the future. That decision of full commitment will bring the mind-set of selflessness, allowing you to offer the greatest love and support for them.

Jeffrey R. Holland said,

> I wish to encourage every one of us regarding the opposition that so often comes after enlightened decisions have been made, after moments of revelation and conviction have given us a peace and an assurance we thought we would never lose. . . . If it was right when you prayed about it and trusted it and lived for it, it is right now. Don't give up when the pressure mounts. Certainly don't give in to that being who is bent on the destruction of your happiness. Face your doubts. Master your fears. "Cast not away therefore your confidence." Stay the course and see the beauty of life unfold for you.[3]

Engaged

Al: We were hiking Ensign Peak, the place where Ben had originally brought up marriage for the first time, and there was a view of the Salt Lake Temple, where our first "date" had been. On the hike down, Ben got on one knee and proposed! I was shocked!

Ben: I proposed without the ring! It wasn't in yet like it was supposed to be, and I was getting frustrated that I couldn't propose to her yet. Then my dad told me that I didn't need to propose with a ring.

Al: I'm not fancy; I told Ben I would be fine to go to Walmart to get a cheap ring, but he wasn't having that!

Ben: I'm not going to get you a cheapo ring for something you'll wear for years. A week or so after I proposed, the ring came in.

Al: It was *really late* at night, and I had just got home from speaking in a city pretty far away. I was exhausted. I put on an oversized shirt, some oversized sweatpants, and made a bowl of cereal, thinking about how awful it was that I had to wake up for work in only a few short hours. Then I heard a knock on the door. *Who on earth is knocking on the door this late?* It was Ben. He looked at me and said, "Babe, put the cereal down." When I came back from the kitchen, Ben was on one knee with the ring, and he proposed again. We just cried.

Ben: I didn't cry; you were the one crying.

Al: You did cry; you cried more than I did. Anyway, we were engaged "officially," announced it to everyone, and then had a wedding to plan for!

Ben: Al and I were always so simple, and we never really needed to spend money to have fun and do things together. So while planning a wedding, we didn't want that to change. We wanted to keep the focus on the sealing and didn't care too much for a fancy reception. Not that a fancy reception is bad; it just wasn't our style.

Al: It was really important to us to keep our wedding focused on the temple and not the reception, and to not spend money that we didn't have. Which, at the time, we didn't have any money at all. Ben was unemployed, and I was only making twelve dollars an hour and had an entire two-bedroom house to myself in Provo. I never did the roommate thing because I was too independent and stubborn to ever like the idea of living with other girls. Most of my money went to the house, or to gas, to drive and speak everywhere. Both of our families were not in good spots financially, and they weren't going to be able to help out in any way, which was totally fine with us! I found my dress online for a low price, and I really don't think we spent over three hundred dollars for our entire wedding, and everything came out great. We were definitely blessed to have people wanting to help us and gift a lot to us. It was a humble wedding, but we loved it and it turned out awesome and stress-free.

The Wedding

Ben: We got married on August 22, 2013, Al's four-year baptism anniversary. It was so great to walk into the sealing room and see my family and all of our friends waiting and smiling. The sealer's name legit was Wilford Woodruff, so that was awesome.

Al: We felt prepared for the sealing because we did sealings together so much before our wedding. Kneeling across that altar, looking at him, I don't think I had ever felt happier in my life.

Ben: It was neat to go to our reception and see how it all came together. It looked great. We were definitely surprised at the turnout of all who came; it was a lot of fun!

Al: Except, so many people came that we didn't get to eat any of the food! I called my mom and dad on the way to Park City, where we were staying that night, because they hadn't been able to come out. That was more than fine because they aren't members, and it would have been hard to see them sit outside the temple and not feel included. Plus, we were going to do a New York reception later that year and do a ring ceremony; I let my mom plan the whole thing, which was her dream come true! A New York reception later on with my family was definitely best-case scenario for me. After calling my family, we finally got to the hotel room. This is it, our honeymoon! We sit on the bed, and we looked into each other's eyes, and Ben said, "Darling, I am starving!"

Ben: Just as quick as we got in, we were out the door to go get food nearby at the Burger King drive-through.

It was the only thing open. And for the rest of the weekend, we stayed and played in Park City. We love it there; it's our escape place to just be outside and have fun.

Al: Just like that, we were married. We became a team.

Transitioning to Marriage

Al: I was already living in our new place a month before we got married. So when we got married, our house was already set up. It's funny because when we were engaged, one of the nights when we were traveling for me to speak, my dog ate my entire bed. Literally. So for the first two months of us being married, we didn't have a bed. We camped out on the floor. It was actually one of our favorite things looking back. I'm not sure why it didn't bother either of us, but it didn't. Buying a bed wasn't even a plan we were working toward. The only reason we ended up getting one was because someone in our ward heard that we were sleeping on the floor, and they went out and bought us one as a surprise and as a welcome-to-the-ward gift. I'm sure they thought it was the worst thing they had ever seen when they saw our sleeping situation.

Ben: Our first house together was a tiny duplex that didn't even have a closet or enough space for a love seat or even a table in any of the rooms. We ate a lot of our meals on the floor because we couldn't fit any chairs, which was fine because we didn't have any anyway. Our new bed took up the entire bedroom, and our door couldn't close all the way.

Al: We loved being together no matter where we were, even if it was in our small house that started to ooze this weird yellow color on one of the walls. We spent so much time together that there were no big surprises when we moved in and finally combined our lives together. It felt completely natural and easy and fairly seamless, which is how it should be, I think. The fewer surprises, the better.

Ben: When you are engaged, it is a time full of excitement. Going home at night and leaving each other is a terrible feeling; you never want to be apart and you long for those times to end. When you first get married, not having those goodbyes at night is one of the most satisfying feelings you'll have. Those first few months or so are almost more exciting than any time you had during your courtship. Then some time goes by, and it settles in that you have all of this downtime together at home that you didn't have before you were married. And now you are, for the most part, together all the time. You're doing things together that you haven't done before, mostly the *small, menial, routine things*. But the transition to marriage can be smooth, even with these new, full-transparency moments that you now have together. Al and I are both really easygoing people and little things just don't bother us, and I think that should be a rule of thumb for marriage. All the big stuff was talked about before we tied the knot, so what was left were those small things we might not have noticed about the other during our courtship. It's just, we all need to be willing to not let which way the toilet paper roll faces bother us.

Al: As smooth as the transition was, there were some things I was worried about on my end because of some of my personality quirks. Independence has always been one of my strongest traits. I never had a problem doing anything on my own, and in fact, would usually prefer it that way. I was, and still am, a little stubborn and if I wanted to do something, I did. I was always nervous about getting married because I didn't know how I could suddenly include someone else with everything. I had been living completely on my own for six years now. I was worried I would have a hard time losing all the alone time I was so used to. On top of my personality quirks, I had a two-bedroom house full of stuff to myself, including an eighty-pound dog, and Ben was now a part of that life. Those worries, although valid, proved to be a waste of time. My independence and all that came with it, those were things that Ben already knew about me. He knew and accepted all of those things. He not only embraced me and everything that I was, but he even took time and looked for ways to support, promote, and make time for those things that I enjoyed doing.

Ben: Being yourself right from the start is absolutely essential. "Start" means while you're dating, not once you're married. We were always ourselves around each other, so those little quirks about ourselves that we worried about when we thought of living together had already surfaced before we even got married.

Al: Other than our oozing house, everything was off to a great start.

And so it begins!

LESSONS WE'VE
LEARNED

Lesson One

It's Not about You

The happiest people I know are those who
lose themselves in the service of others.
—Gordon B. Hinckley[4]

A selfless person is one who is more concerned about the
happiness and well-being of another than about his or her
own convenience or comfort, one who is willing to serve
another when it is neither sought for nor appreciated. . . .
A selfless person displays a willingness to sacrifice, a
willingness to purge from his or her mind and heart
personal wants, and needs, and feelings.
—H. Burke Peterson[5]

When we were engaged and being interviewed for our sealing recommend, Al's stake president looked Ben in the eye and told him, "You are selfish." Our eyes bugged out when he said this. We were a bit taken aback, but Al's stake president followed his statement with a smile. He continued to explain that throughout everyone's lives everyone has been selfish. We, as people, have mostly thought of ourselves every day: we wear what we want to wear, we eat what we want to eat, and we do what we want to do when we want to do it. We get in the mind-set of "me, me, me," and unconsciously listen to our immediate needs and desires.

Her stake president then leaned forward and locked eyes with Ben, saying, "Ben, it's all about her." But almost immediately, he then looked into Al's eyes, and said the same thing, "Al, from now on, it is all about him."

We left the interview excited because we were one signature closer to being sealed, but we also left with a feeling of responsibility for each other and the decision we were making. We realized and really felt that from now on, it's not about us. It's about serving them. This was the start of learning what we think is one of the most important lessons in marriage: it's all about *them*.

The Little Things

Often we assume that they must know how
much we love them. But we should never assume; we
should let them know. Wrote William Shakespeare,
'They do not love that do not show their love.' We will never
regret the kind words spoken or the affection shown. Rather,
our regrets will come if such things are omitted from our
relationships with those who mean the most to us.
—Thomas S. Monson[6]

Al: I was having a terrible day at work one day. It was
one of those days that seemed to be never-ending and
where everything was going wrong. I was desperate
to leave and go home. Yet at the same time, I was in
a bad mood and wanted to be alone, so the idea of
being home and being "with it" to be with Ben and
help with our kids seemed hard too. I walked through
our front door, threw my stuff on the ground, and
before I could say or do anything else, Ben came up
to me, pulled me into his chest, and kissed me on
the forehead. Before I could unload about how bad
my day had been, and before I even had a chance to
break down crying, he grabbed both of my hands and
started slow dancing in our kitchen. He dipped me
and said, "Hey, beautiful, I'm so glad you're home.
Dinner is in the oven." Well, shoot. So much for my
plans of a pity party and sulking in our bedroom. To
no surprise, whatever I was flustered about seemed

to not to matter as much anymore. Not enough to ruin my night. Not enough to stop me from smiling, being happy, playing with our kids, and joking with Ben.

Love is very much, in other words, serving. And service does not have to be big, planned, or well thought out. It's about going through your every day and thinking, *What can I do that will help them out or make them smile? What can I do so that they know I'm thinking of them?* Because I'm not sure that we'd find anyone who said a random text from their spouse saying, "I freaking love you," didn't make their day. I'm not sure we'd find someone that said a surprise forehead kiss didn't melt their heart. I'm not sure we'd find someone that said they didn't like unexpected compliments.

When we reflect on how we know the other loves us, Al would say that she knows because Ben cuts up vegetables for her lunch the night before without her asking, and Ben knows because Al never judges him when he nervously paces the floor throughout an entire LSU football game or when he sings Shania Twain in the shower. It's the little things.

Love is *actively* thinking about the other person. Love is doing things for them without being told to. We're not saying it's not important to tell the other your expectations or what you'd like help with, but we are saying to look for ways to serve on your own too. Love is seeing them fold laundry—not because you asked them to, but because they saw a need. Love is buying their favorite candy bar at the store when you were only going there for diapers. Love is waiting to watch your favorite show on Netflix until you're both together. Love is *very much* those random texts. Love is laughing at the awkward and not judging for the embarrassing. Love is including them in your personal prayers, and it is acting on those small ideas that pop into your head.

Real love is when you become selfless. . . .
You're now a giver instead of a taker.
—Sylvester Stallone[7]

Arguments

Arguments and disagreements are bound to happen; it's natural. You are two different people with two different personalities and ideas and backgrounds. A lot of the "arguments" we've had, we usually find out that they are, in the bigger picture, insignificant things. Actively thinking, *Does this even matter in the scheme of things?* while you're in an argument helps end things that maybe should have never started in the first place. If you find you're arguing over something small, it is absolutely more than okay to start laughing at yourself and at the situation. Chances are, if it is truly insignificant, your spouse doesn't want to be fighting about it either. It is more than okay to apologize and just stop it right then.

In arguments that do matter, it's a lot of how we personally choose to react in those situations that can affect the type of experience it's going to be. Often, it's a whole lot of reacting to the other person that makes up the experience. If either of us is screaming, then, naturally, the other one usually starts yelling too. We've had our share of kicked boxes, slammed doors, and tears of frustration, all of which were results of misunderstandings, overreactions, moments of pride, or times when there was a lack of communication.

Destructive damage comes from faultfinding, blame, and guilt. It is absolutely not useful to point out whose fault something is. Instead, be productive by accepting that it has already happened, and spend time and effort working together to fix it or move past it.

Al: When Gracie was two, she and Ben were playing rough in the living room, and Ben was bouncing her on his knee too close to the coffee table. His leg slipped, and she fell and whacked her face on the table, knocking out her front tooth. A trip to the ER and Gracie not having a front tooth for the next seven or eight years came from it. Even though I may have thought it a few times in my head, I never told him that this wouldn't have happened if it weren't for him playing too rough and that it was all his fault. Our first year of marriage, however, I would have. But I learned early on, *the hard way*, that situations already stink without having me add blame on top of them.

It would have just caused separation (or maybe resentment) between us, and the situation could have been much worse. Intentionally putting your spouse down is *never* justified or acceptable. Ben already felt bad enough as it was, and placing blame on him wouldn't have helped in any way. Instead, we made a bad situation better and smoother simply by avoiding those statements and thoughts, and instead saying to each other, "Okay, *we*," (not singling him out by saying "you") "won't play that close to the table anymore because that really sucked and we don't want that to happen again."

It's easy to put our feelings before our spouse's when we're upset. And when we're upset, we want them to know we're upset usually before we even ask about how they're feeling. But our feelings are *not* any more important or any more valid than theirs. Remembering that we are a team is really important. And even though what you're feeling is *real* and valid to *you*, what they are feeling is *real* and valid to *them*. Even if you don't understand them, letting them talk, vent, or share their feelings first can help you see where they are coming from.

But mostly, we've found that it's a crucial make-or-break thing to say a prayer with each other, no matter how frustrated we are. Then the Spirit is with us. Then we are thinking about the other's feelings, and an understanding happens. Then we avoid name-calling or saying things we don't mean. Then our arguments just turn into productive *conversations.* We realize that arguments don't *have* to happen if we decide that we don't want them to. It's tricky sometimes; we totally get it. But if you decide to turn to God every time an argument comes up, it's easier to allow Him to help you communicate and avoid the unnecessary burdens.

Ben: There are times when I come home frustrated from school or just flat-out had a rough day, and I will develop a tone. I become negative, and at times that negativity is unintentionally directed at my wife. She hasn't done anything wrong, or said anything rude; I just take my frustration out on her simply because she is there. It is foolish of me every time. It's a flaw of mine. At times, I don't even notice the tone in my voice, but Al always points it out, and I love that about her. She'll say, "Hey, your tone," or, "Babe, easy." Or my favorite, "Check yourself before you wreck yourself." When she says those things, sometimes I roll my eyes or get more frustrated, but because she lets me know, I stop to realize how I am acting. Before I know it, we're laughing and I forget all about what was bothering me. Most of our arguments are over foolish things that don't even really matter, but one in particular started from having a long, busy day when I got upset with my wife because she didn't make a decision for dinner.

The thing is, I wasn't making the decision on what to cook and eat either. We were both bothered, tired, and hangry: the deadly triple threat. We got so frustrated that we started to argue with each other—all over what? Food? I have learned and relearned how to better handle myself in those situations. My wife is the type of person that needs a minute to be alone when we have our disagreements. She likes to be able to go and say a prayer, calm down, and remove herself momentarily from the situation to avoid overreacting or saying something she doesn't mean.

At first, it was tough because I'm the exact opposite. When problems arise, I like to talk them out right away and not sit in silence by myself. I've had to learn to give her space to think things over. We've found what works for us, and that's giving each other that short time to regroup. She comes out of the room, and the situation turns to immediate forgiveness. "Babe, I'm sorry for how I was acting. Please forgive me." "Sweetheart, I was being dumb." "Let's make out instead."

Forgiveness is already given to each other before it's even asked for. When I give her a short time in a separate room, and as I sit by myself, I tend to realize how much of a schmuck I was and where I need to improve as a person and a husband. Forgiveness needs be a huge part of relationships. Mistakes are going to happen. Forgive your spouse when problems come up and arguments occur. I'm thankful my wife always forgives me because it makes me love her so much more, realizing that she sees through my imperfections and the mistakes I make. She makes me want to be better for her.

I read a quote once from President Thomas S. Monson, where he said: "Men, take care not to make women weep, for God counts their tears."[8] I try to remember that every time I'm frustrated or when troubles arise, and it helps in those situations to make sure I never hurt my wife or her feelings.

Forgiveness

Arguments last longer when we hold on to how we are feeling and only think that our feelings and views are right or justified above the other person's. Looking back on our disagreements, they were almost always due to our individual, ignorant, prideful, and selfish mind-sets. We have learned that our personal feelings and views need to be momentarily pushed aside to let the other person talk, explaining their feelings, so we can better understand their views. To love is to forgive. No matter what you're arguing about, the best thing to do is sincerely apologize. You may be thinking, *Yeah, but I didn't do anything wrong,* or *It was all their fault.* It doesn't matter. Already have it in your mind and in your heart that you will move past what you are currently in. And when an argument is settled and forgiven, it must truly be over.

Bringing it up again in future arguments is destructive. It is easier to talk and be open with your spouse in a future disagreement when you know they will not bring up past arguments and mistakes. Al's dad wrote in our wedding card, "It's great to be good *for* each other, but it is more important to be good *to* each other."

Lastly, there's this, and it is an art, but it's a craft that we suggest everyone learn: Get. Over. It. Yep. Three powerful action words. It takes a lot of time, a lot of focus, and a lot of practice. But it's something that was a game changer once we figured it out. With little tiffs and frustrations, or the big-gun fights, learn the art of getting over it as quickly as you can.

Small example, when you write a book together with your spouse, it's almost implied that you won't have the same vision on some parts, or will spend too many hours day in and day out on the book and will get frustrated and accidentally take it out on each other, simply because you're together. Just barely, we got frustrated over something stupid while sitting at our kitchen table writing this after too many hours of working on it. We both recognized it at the same time, and we both got up; Ben went and put on a movie for the kids and Al raided the fridge. We came back to the table minutes later, at the same time, on our own, and with a clear mind. We both apologized, and just like that, we went on writing as if it didn't even happen. It didn't come that easy at first, but man is it refreshing to do that!

Al: Every time we have had an argument, it has always ended the same. It usually takes me longer to push my pride aside and see things from his side, and I'm usually the last to apologize. Ben's response is always genuinely, "I already forgave you." It has always been that way, and it still does completely surprise me how he could forgive me before my apology comes. He always has forgiveness in his heart—in every single situation—before the yelling even stops. The quicker we can apologize, the quicker the other will apologize too, and the quicker we can both realize that we are acting silly. Then we can both move on from it and have more time for stuff we actually like doing. 'Cause ain't nobody likes fighting.

Pride

The counsel from Al's stake president, "It's all about them," is a direct way of addressing pride. And the funny thing about pride is that it's easy to detect in others, but we rarely detect it in ourselves. Overcoming pride is about going back to those questions we should be asking ourselves every day, like, "How can I make my spouse's life easier? How can I show them I love them?"

Al: When Christian was eight months old, he went through this weird week-and-a-half-long phase of not sleeping *at all*. It was terrible. And the worst part was that before this, he had slept through the night since he was a newborn, so we were completely unadjusted to it. Both of us were completely exhausted, getting no sleep at all, and were trying to handle this situation in a mostly unconscious state. In the daze we were in, we were screaming at each other.

To say I was upset, frustrated, and short-tempered is the understatement of the century. Other than exhausted, I was bitter because I had to go to work in the morning while Ben had a chance of napping later when the kids did. One of the nights during this awful week, I was so tired and frustrated and I knew—and didn't even care—that I was yelling and being completely over the top. Once Christian had finally calmed down and had fallen back asleep, for good this time, I had to start getting ready for work in thirty minutes. In my living-dead frustration, I directed my anger at Ben and made sure he knew that somehow all of this was his fault. During my yelling and blaming, happening while I was lying down with my eyes closed, half asleep, and slurring my words, Ben didn't say anything back. He just climbed in bed and he held me. Not in a way that said he wasn't listening, but he held me tight, responding in a way that no words could have done. And I learned several awfully crucial lessons in that exact moment. Love is understanding and selflessness. Love is forgiveness and moving past things. And love is actively thinking of them—not yourself.

As you move forward with marriage, it will no longer be about "I" and "Me," but will always and forever be "Us" and "We." Let's not let anything come in the way of loving our spouse and putting them before our selfish desires. It is always better to be kind and understanding than to be right. Let's lose ourselves in them and, no matter what happens, be there for them. Forgive quickly and always. Every day, let's wake up and think of what we can do to make things easier for them. Learn and love their quirks. Every day, let's love fully and selflessly. Embrace and accept the differences we have. Act and react knowing that we are both on equal ground with our spouse. As we forgive, accept, and become more selfless, we will be surprised and humbled by how they will treat us in return. Strength and fluidity will be added to your marriage, and then you will have more time to laugh and be happy.

Lesson Two

Communication

Every couple, whether in the first or the twenty-first
year of marriage, should discover the value of
pillow-talk time at the end of the day.
—Robert L. Simpson[9]

Good communication includes taking time to
plan together. Couples need private time to observe,
to talk, and really listen to each other.
—Russell M. Nelson[10]

The way we communicate with others and the
way we communicate with ourselves ultimately
determine the quality of our lives.
—Anthony Robbins[11]

Constant communication is one of the most vital needs for a marriage to become and remain strong. Without it, there will be harder roadblocks, struggles, and separations. Open communication should be established day one when you first meet each other. There should be no make-or-break surprises surfacing after you kiss over the altar. Know each other's likes, dislikes, struggles, bad habits, and addictions before then. This kind of communication—of being open and honest—is essential so that any major problems or concerns can be addressed before marriage. We also need to know and understand exactly where they are in terms of their testimony of the gospel. Learn and get to know what their triggers are, and how to tell when something is on their mind and is bothering them.

Once you are married and live together, there's a lot of time to notice the little things about your spouse that you never got to see before. You see how they are all the time. You see how they are when there is no one is around. Not only are they completely themselves, but you are completely yourself, and all your imperfections and quirks are exposed.

Communication during marriage should never stop. It's more important—now more than ever—to keep those lines open, to allow your communication to continue to be successful and functioning. We must always be open with our spouse about everything. We cannot have any fears about talking to them and letting them know how we feel.

Marriage will always bring decisions, emotions, and arguments that need both spouses' cooperation.

We know a married couple whom we love and admire. They have been married for over fifteen years and have a wonderful family. They are a great example of how love and communication should work. But apparently, early on in their marriage, it wasn't so easy. The husband, Pete (name changed), had struggled with pornography as a teenager. It was a terrible habit. He thought this habit was gone, but shortly after he and his wife were married, his pornography issue resurfaced, and it became a problem he couldn't shake on his own. He tried for months to quit without help, but he still struggled. If he wanted to overcome pornography, he knew he would need his wife's help. He was embarrassed, ashamed, and afraid to even bring it up to her. What would she say? How would she react? Would she leave him?

When he told his wife, she obviously was upset and hurt. She had never known that he had this struggle. But she was willing to listen to him. Pete admitted how foolish and wrong he was and how he *wanted* to overcome it, but he needed her help. He couldn't do it without her. She saw his humility and his sincerity. Even though she was upset with him, she loved him and was willing to help him overcome this addiction because of his willingness to change. It was important for Pete to receive this help from his wife, and it was important for his wife to feel needed, wanted, and included in this situation and to seek the help he needed *together*. They were able to overcome this problem together.

Years have flown by since they had this issue: they have had children, their love and intimacy is strong, and they are thriving. They credit this experience as helping them grow closer together early on in their marriage.

For Pete's sake (no pun intended), he should have told his wife about his past struggles with pornography when they were dating, even if it wasn't an issue at the time. Transparency brings trust. Admittedly, he was embarrassed and thought he could manage it alone, but by not communicating with his wife, he caused more hurt and surprise. Don't be afraid to bring up your problems or things you may personally struggle with. The person you love needs to know these things; they can help, and if it's out of their hands, you can both seek out professional help. When someone you love tells you their problems and admits their struggles, it is productive and healthy to not judge them, but seek to understand and help them.

What should we do when someone tells us, before we're married, about an addiction they have or had? Should it be a deal breaker? Sister Carole M. Stephens had the perfect response to this, "'What's in the heart? Are you dating someone who has a good heart, who's honest about it, who is willing to work with you, who is willing to take the 12-step course and to really study the scriptures?' she asked, 'Can you work through this together?'"[12] She related this to when Alma counseled his son Corianton, who had not kept the law of chastity.

Quoting Alma 48:17–18, she read,

> If all men had been, and were, and ever would be, like unto Moroni, behold, the very powers of hell would have been shaken forever; yea, the devil would never have power over the hearts of the children of men.
>
> Behold, he was a man like unto Ammon, the son of Mosiah, yea, and even the other sons of Mosiah, yea, and also Alma and his sons, for *they were all men of God.* (Italics added)

Sister Stephens pointed out how this scripture doesn't say "'Alma and his sons, except for Corianton.' It lists him among those who are 'like unto Moroni.'"[13] She counseled that it isn't necessarily the person's sin that we should make our decision by, it's their heart. Are they honest about it? Are they wanting to change? The Atonement is very real and can help heal and change those who actively and willingly use it.

What to Communicate About

One of the biggest things we've learned about communication is being able to express how we feel in the moment and not letting it build up and become an issue. Keeping things to yourself and letting feelings build up can cause so many problems. We shouldn't expect or assume that our spouse can read our minds when something is wrong. Not talking to them prolongs the lack of advice, love, and relief.

We've both had to learn to get things off our chest as soon as they come up, rather than waiting and not saying anything. Everything you feel and go through matters. On the other hand, don't be afraid to ask your spouse if something is wrong if they are not coming to you. Be aware, and know when your spouse gets bothered or in a mood, so you can be quick to help.

Al: I can always tell when something is bothering Ben because he always gets really quiet. Usually, when I ask, he'll respond that there's nothing wrong or there's nothing to talk about. That's when I make him sit down and just flat out say, "I can tell something's on your mind, what's up," and I'll sit by him until we can talk about it. He does the same thing with me as well. While we work incredibly well together with the bigger decisions and the large issues going on in our lives, I sometimes don't want to bring up something I think is too small or too silly. I usually get quiet and start cleaning a lot out of nowhere. What I have learned, and have had to relearn, a lot in the beginning of our marriage is that I have never bothered Ben by telling him what is on my mind, and nothing is too small to bring up to him.

I'm not sure why it was so difficult for me whenever something like this came up, because absolutely every time I have addressed even the smallest of things to him, I have received the greatest advice and comfort; I am able to move past the issue quicker than if I had kept it to myself. Realizing that God uses your spouse to help you in the ways you need makes not turning to them seem incredibly silly.

Heavenly Father answers our prayers a lot of the time through other people. When we get married, our spouse is usually the primary responder to and caregiver of our prayers. Our spouses are inspired to know how to help and comfort us, in the greatest way that we need them to, because that is the purpose of a companion: to be a helpmeet.

Life is hard. There are going to be a lot of trials, tests, and big decisions to be made that will require work and faith. The power of combined faith will be what gets you through the toughest times. But, as we know, enduring to the end and staying strong is difficult. Discussions about where you are and what you are struggling with will change, and those issues will need to be discussed frequently and openly. When we open up about what's on our minds and allow our spouse to be aware of those things, they can more quickly help and work on them with us.

Spiritual

Spiritual strength and compatibility are important principles to a successful marriage, and they are what will help you both through the hard times you'll face. They will also build your connection, as a couple, closer together as a whole. We have learned that the most crucial thing to talk about *before* and during marriage is the gospel and where we are in terms of our individual testimonies. God must always stay the biggest part of the relationship because it's from Him that we get the greatest help, understanding, and love. It cannot be just a Sunday thing. As a couple, we personally have mini devotionals with each other daily. (And we do mean *mini.*) We are there to build up, strengthen, and take care of each other, and the best way to do that is to spiritually feed our souls. Marriage needs the Spirit, and the best way to bring the Spirit to the two of you—together as a unit—is to talk about spiritual things. Tell each other what stood out to you from reading scriptures: tell them your thoughts, impressions, ideas, and revelations. It doesn't need to be a big thing that takes planning. Talk about it at dinner, or in the car, or text each other a scripture of the day. Practice doing this every day so it's comfortable and common between the two of you and becomes a daily habit. As long as it's happening, and you're making it a daily habit, then you will always be building a connection between the two of you as a *team.*

It is also crucial to tell each other your questions, struggles, and spiritual shortcomings. It is incredibly important that your spouse knows where you stand, what is on your mind, and what questions you may have, so they can help you. It's totally okay to have questions, but it is not okay to do nothing about them and postpone resolving them. Unresolved struggles or questions turn into a slippery slope with the adversary. Having your spouse there to help you grow and become better makes things *so* much easier. We don't need to do things alone and we're not meant to. We're meant to help each other become who God wants us to be, to do the things He has set out for us to do, and to help each other get home *together*.

Al: There have been times where one or both of us are having a hard time with something, and it has been the biggest help and blessing to let the other one know about it. That added help and motivation or accountability helps us to do better with it. For example, sometimes Ben skips his morning prayer to take me to work because he wakes up too late and has to jump in the car right then to get me to work on time. He came to me and told me that something he wants to do better with is not missing his morning prayers. Since he told me that, now I say, "Hey, did you talk to God yet this morning? Totally waiting before we leave so you can." And he'll do the same for me with whatever I need to work on as well.

Expectations

It's crucial to talk about expectations *before* you're married. Because nothing will be more of a surprise and a challenge than getting married and realizing that your ideals, expectations, and goals are completely different from each other. Moving forward together will be harder when you both have different ideas of what direction you want to be moving in. What are your future goals? Do you both want to be working toward the same things for your future? Do your views of each other's roles in a marriage match up? If not, are they small enough differences to compromise and tailor to each other? What things are a must for you?

Maybe we don't need an example of what happens when we don't communicate our expectations; maybe we can fill in the blanks ourselves. To those that are single, express your expectations before you're married. It will save you both a lot of grief down the line.

It's been hard to see a friend of Al's fall in love, get married in the temple, and from day one have a really hard marriage. Once they were together all the time and working toward their future expectations of what life would be like, they discovered that what they were building and working toward was different from each other. When they were dating, they didn't make it much further in their conversations than the fact that they wanted to get married in the temple. And they did. Her expectations were that he would be dressed up all the time, they would always be out doing things with her high school friends, and church was optional and not that big of deal when missed. When they were home together, she preferred spending all of her time on her phone texting her friends and planning their next outing. His expectations were, let's just say, different. They struggled for a few years, and ultimately their marriage ended in a divorce. They didn't want the same things. They didn't want to work toward one another's goals.

Expressing expectations should be a habit we do on small and large scales every day. Expectations not just for things that are overall and long-term, but for the day-to-day expectations as well. What expectations do you have for each other today? If you come home from work and expect the dishes to be done, it isn't too logical to get mad at your spouse when the dishes aren't done if you never expressed that expectation to them. How were they to know?

Growth and fluidity also come from expressing the daily expectations we have for *ourselves* to our spouse, so they can help us. You should have expectations as a couple, as parents, at work, in callings, and of course, as disciples who should be actively serving God. While expectations are natural and can be positive, it's when they are not communicated and not met by someone else that brings heartache.

Intimacy

Intimacy is a piece of the puzzle that is needed to complete a healthy marriage. It's a level of connection that is created *by God* to bind you both closer together in ways that other things can't. All we're going to say in this section (because we talk more about intimacy in the next chapter) is to *communicate* with each other about this. It can be a weird dynamic for some to grow up and not really talk about intimacy at all—just knowing the things you can't do until you're married. And then being married, and having to learn with your spouse how to talk about it, feel comfortable with it, and know that it is absolutely natural and essential. Tell each other your expectations. Tell each other what you like, what you don't like, and what you're comfortable with. Don't be embarrassed; be transparent and open. This should absolutely be enjoyable for both of you, *together*, so communicate to always make sure that it is.

Al: Not just "bedroom" stuff either; small things go a long way and everything should be communicated. Telling the other what's on your mind is much easier than feeling distanced or unhappy. I'll flat out tell Ben that I don't think we've kissed enough that day. Or if I've had a bad day, I'll tell him how just rubbing my back will help. And he'll do it because I've asked him to. Side note: Guys, when in doubt, rub your wife's back, anyway. It is always a good idea.

Finance

Looking at the world as a whole, money is primarily what brings the most grief to a marriage. We live in a world where money is the driving force behind everything. It's competitive; you can easily compare yourself to your neighbors or friends and wish you were making as much money as them. You should never be so focused on money that you lose focus on what matters most. Obviously, money is important; we have to have it to survive. Bills need to be paid and food needs to be bought.

Finances should be communicated early and often in your marriage, and ideally before marriage. We aren't going to tell you the best way to handle your money because it will be different for everyone. But we are telling you that it's something you do need to figure out and agree on together. Get a system that works for you. We have found that combining our accounts together into one works best for us. Finances should never be kept as secrets or become competitive within companionships. It's not "my" money or "his" or "her" money; it is, and will forever be, "our" money.

Ben: Being a team with money was something I had to learn early on in our marriage. The first year of us being together, I bounced from interview to interview and job to job. I have turned down so many job opportunities because they didn't feel right; I made a decision long ago to never say yes to something that doesn't feel right, no matter how tempting it may be. It may seem foolish to some, but let me tell you, it would have been foolish if I was doing something knowing that it was wrong and that it wasn't what God wanted me to do.

When school came up for me, Al and I made the decision that I should just focus on that. Al had already graduated from school and had—and still has—a career with a great salary, so there wasn't any pressure for me to work. At the time though, it was difficult for me to accept the fact that Al would be the breadwinner of the family. As a man, pride kicked in, and I spent most of my time wishing I had a career job like her. I would often compare myself to her and her salary, and it would bother me. When I would get frustrated, Al would always remind me by saying, "Babe, it's nothing. This is ours." Seeing how it didn't bother her that I was a full-time student helped me realize how marriage becomes a team effort in every field. Seeing her love me, as a dedicated student, and having her tell me, "Don't worry about it, it's our money. Besides, when you're finished with school, it will be you who will be the main provider for me and our family." We set a goal while on our honeymoon to never let money become an issue. Knowing that we have that goal makes it easier to communicate about money and not stress about it.

Now, we realize that not every marriage is like ours, and sometimes both of you need to work and that is perfectly fine. Just be sure to address money, jobs, debts, salaries, and roles before marriage. This way, there won't be any financial surprises or confusion when you are married. Be willing to work together and use your money as a team.

Live within your means, have a budget, and set goals. We tend to budget every paycheck and list when our bills are due so that we know what we have and what we need to pay. Be open about finances, and don't let money bruise or damage your marriage. Don't keep purchases secret from your spouse because you're worried about how they'll react when they see the receipt. The pursuit of money can be destructive, but in marriage, the lack of communication about finances can be even more damaging.

Emotional Infidelity

Communication is needed between spouses. But we should also be aware of communication that *shouldn't* necessarily be happening as well. Not with each other, but with other people that may be inappropriate or hurtful. Being too friendly or flirtatious is dangerous. There is no such thing as "harmless" flirting. Be aware of how you communicate with others, and the language you use. Anything that could make your spouse uncomfortable should cease.

LDS.org came out with a really amazing article that articulates what exactly emotional infidelity entails. We'll share a few things.

> In some ways, these types of emotional connections are more harmful than physical connections. Betrayed partners often report more distress about a spouse's emotional involvement with someone outside the marriage than about the physical betrayal that often follows. In the words of one client, "I believe that my wife loves me, but I also believe that a sliver of her heart belongs to him, and I can't live with that." . . .
>
> Be especially careful in your online contact with former love interests, since previous familiarity

potentially ignites high levels of emotion, says [researcher] Dr. Glass. People are often unprepared for the emotion elicited from these encounters and can misinterpret the feelings to mean that the old bond is somehow more legitimate than the marriage relationship. This comparison is inaccurate and fraudulent. While brain chemicals produced in these situations are real and drug-like, they are also fleeting and unsustainable. . . .

People tend to be more open about sharing intimate feelings. This creates intense emotional connections. Some feel like they can have the novelty of infidelity online with one person while enjoying the stability of marriage in real life with another. This plan does not work. Infidelity in any of its forms compromises marriages spiritually, structurally, and sometimes irreparably.[14]

Another level of this occurs when our spouse is not the first person we turn to about things. When our spouse isn't the first person we call with exciting news, or if they aren't the first person we open up to about a struggle, or if they aren't the one we are talking to about a struggle—even if the struggle is with your spouse—then changes should be made. Most commonly, under the term of emotional infidelity, it is with someone of the opposite sex, but don't overlook any relationship that comes *before your spouse*—including our parents.

Al: This is kind of an extreme example, but a friend of mine had a wife who struggled with this. She called her parents for everything, and I mean everything. Unfortunately, anytime she was struggling with something or needed advice, her husband was never her first option. When she had a disagreement with her husband, she didn't talk to him and work it out; she left. She would literally leave the house all the time and go home to her mom. Sometimes, my friend would wake up in the morning and she would be gone and hadn't told him. As you can imagine, there was a huge disconnect between my friend and his wife. This brought heartache to him in several ways and a long list of unresolved problems that started to stack up. These problems could have been avoided had they just turned to each other first and communicated and worked their problems out as they were happening. Unfortunately, their marriage ended because of the separation created between them.

How to Make More Time to Communicate

We live in a time when it is a lot easier and faster to text than talk. Between TV and Instagram, video games and tablets, there are too many gadgets that fight for our attention. And after a short time being married, it's easy to take for granted the time you spend with your spouse and use all those things that can so easily take you away from them.

Once we got married and settled into our new place, we had Internet at our home, something we had seldom used while we were dating. There was schoolwork to do and blogs to write, and it was great to be able to do those things from home. But then, we started to take advantage of it and got a little carried away. We didn't communicate as often during the night hours because it seemed we always found something to "work on." What it came down to was, we were just wasting time online together. Time slipped away and before we knew it, we were going to bed. We realized that we weren't spending our time home together properly, and even though we were together, we weren't really together.

Knowing that we needed and wanted to make a change, we made a plan to not use any technology before 9 p.m. every night. We called it "unplugged" time. It made a huge difference in our relationship. We would do so many more things together: cooking, going on walks, playing games, being with our dogs, and just enjoying each other. It quickly got to the point where we forgot about our "unplugged" time frame because it became a habit; we loved to interact with each other. Our desires shifted, and we started setting good goals and realizing every day how cool we both still are. We made plans that Ben would finish all his homework at school, and Al would leave her work at work and not bring it home, so that when we were together, we were *together*. Time waits for no man, or to use a line from a hymn, "Time flies on wings of lightning; we cannot call it back."[15]

When you go out to eat, try not to spend your time on your phones. When we're out together, the rule is no phones at the table so that we can talk and joke and draw ugly pictures while waiting for our food. Every time we go out, we see couples—married or dating—sit at the table both looking down at their screens the entire time. They are missing time to really connect, laugh, and be funny together, or have meaningful conversations. Spending time with someone doesn't count when you don't speak to each other. It doesn't count when you're experiencing different things on your phones and are mentally in different places from each other. Setting goals and guidelines for "unplugged" time in order to stay engaged with each other will be what keeps your interest in each other alive, just like when you first met.

Marriage is not all lovey-dovey; you need time to connect through words and conversation. Don't take one another for granted just because you live with each other.

Ben: Back when Al was speaking six days a week, and we would travel all over, four to six hours away, we somehow never played any music (unless it was karaoke of Michael Jackson or Justin Timberlake). We would just talk and play games the whole time. I have never met anyone with as much of a spontaneous spirit as my wife has. She is so on-the-spot silly and outgoing that there has never been a dull moment with her. I'm glad I was blessed with her because she can make anything, or any situation, one to remember.

Long car rides are our jam. It's like, a thing of ours. Our best conversations happen in the car. A lot of the time, even now with our kids, we take the long way home just so we have more time to talk—no joke. When we're eating dinner, we eat at the table—we don't allow phones or have the TV on—and we talk. Every Sunday after church, we have a prayer and a weekly family counsel where we plan what is coming up that week including things that need to happen, goals we have, expectations, and suggestions. We go on family walks, which is where a lot of our best ideas come from. The time we spend talking together is when promptings come to both of us. We have inside jokes together, and our funniest stories come from these times.

Whether it is financial, spiritual, embarrassing, or whatever might seem small or insignificant, always be open with your spouse. Don't be afraid to talk to them and let them know how you feel. There should be no secrets between you two, and always find time to talk. If you feel like you need to do better with this, fix it. It's important; it's everything in a marriage. Communication in a marriage is what feeds it and keeps it alive. Lack of communication is what causes problems. And who wants problems that could have been avoided? Talk to each other on what changes can be made to better understand and grow closer to each other. You will be happier, and your marriage will be stronger and healthier.

LESSON THREE

Always Have Time for Love

Love is really spelled *t-i-m-e*.
—Dieter F. Uchtdorf[16]

Life is difficult for everyone. Finding ways to make life meaningful and purposeful and rewarding, doing the activities that you love and spending time with the people that you love—I think that's the meaning of this human experience.
—Steve Gleason[17]

Disappointment can quickly come when "things" come before or get in the way of time together. "If we don't have time for love, we're doing something wrong." This was one of the first things that we learned on our own together. After the honeymoon, life starts up again. Just as we found out that our mobile devices were taking up our time, we also learned that things like work, school, and homework easily distracted, or took away from, our affection and attention toward each other. Our spouse should always come first, and dating should last throughout all our years of marriage.

We had received counsel from both of our stake presidents to do everything together whenever possible; we call it the "grocery store" metaphor. Even those menial chores and tasks that need to get done can be a time for us to bond. We made it a priority to follow the counsel given and to not be away from each other, especially with the everyday things. There of course will be times that we can't do everything together, or times when it would make more sense to do some shopping while the other is not home, but our rule of thumb is that if we are home with each other, we do things as a team. Even going to the store.

Dating

Marriage is the best time to date, and it's important to do it consistently to keep the bond between you and your spouse alive and strong. Always keep the dating life that you had before your marriage going, no matter your age or how long you've been together. It's having those fun times together that made you two fall in love, and it will be those things that help you stay in love. At least once a week, we go out and do something out of the house. Frequently, we decide to go to the temple and then go out to dinner after (something about the temple makes us really crave pancakes). Aside from our temple dates, we usually have another night every week that we try to go out to eat someplace new. We love tacos! Okay, that's an understatement. It's an obsession. So we usually try to find a new Mexican restaurant to eat at. Before it went out of business, and this is going to date us a little, we were avid Blockbuster renters (we don't want to talk about it; we're still genuinely sad about them going out of business). We also like looking for free museums and random hole-in-the-wall restaurants in small cities we've never been to; we have found all of our favorite foods that way. Or sometimes we like to go to random hotels to stay for the night and just swim and sightsee. The things that you enjoyed doing together while you were dating, no matter what they may be—keep doing them! Over time, find new things to add too. Date nights when you're married are more fun anyway, because no one gets dropped off afterward and you can go home together.

Al: One time, just to go out and be together, we went to a hotel that was two hours away in a really small town that really only had a diner. It wasn't the cleanest place; it smelled pretty bad; their pool had a nasty

83

black line along the top of the water line; and their "hot breakfast" was small, stale mini muffins stuffed in an even smaller Tupperware. We look back on that time together as one of our favorite memories because it was so random and funny. Although it was probably the grossest place we'd ever stayed in, we'll never forget it, and it was a time that we laughed the hardest and enjoyed each other the most.

There's something about going somewhere or trying something new with Ben that really brings us closer together. My favorite memories that we have together are when we are out of the house doing whatever. I'd hate to think that those memories could have been replaced with wasted time spent doing the "same old, same old."

Quality Time at Home

It is important to have time for yourself and to do those hobbies that you love. Ben likes doing active stuff like hiking or working out, reading self-improvement books, and working on his personal growth, so he'll make time for that. Al loves to be outside, write, and run on the treadmill. We have our separate time to do those things that we love. But when it's just the two of you at the house and you have "nothing" to do, take advantage of your time together. It's times when we find ourselves idling away our time surfing the web, staring at our Instagram feed, or focusing time on other people's lives through social media that we should be thinking about what else can we be doing. If you play video games, play them with your spouse. Read books together, go hiking, talk to each other. It doesn't matter what you do, just do it together!

We learned right off the bat that we couldn't go out all the time now that we're married because we'd go broke *real* quickly. So, we adapted to our new circumstances of married life and came up with new things to try and new activities to do; activities that we now love. Though we weren't necessarily leaving the house to do something, we wanted our time home together to be productive. We developed a passion for and addiction to board games. We, like most, do our share of Netflix and chill, which, for us, is actually just watching *The Office* every night.

One day, when we didn't have anything planned, we ended up learning the entire dance routine to Drake's song, "Hotline Bling." We've gotten more use out of our daughter's Little Tikes basketball hoop than she does, and we play extreme H-O-R-S-E games against each other.

When we're home, we want to *be home*. We want to interact with each other, and give each other the time we need to connect and grow. We try our very best for Al to leave her work at work, and for Ben to try and get all of his homework done before she's home. There are times when that doesn't work, obviously, and that's fine, but it has definitely paid off to have the mind-set of getting it all done previously in order to open our time up for family time.

Affection

Al's stake president told us, "I've been to a lot of sealings where I have seen these little peck kisses."

He continues, "Ben, grab your wife and give her a real kiss at the altar. I don't want to see any of this little 'peck' stuff." And we did just that. Afterward, Ben looked over to see Al's stake president, with a proud look on his face, give Ben a thumbs-up.

Ben: I never had a problem with kissing. In first grade, I was called to the principal's office for playing kissing tag. On my first date with Al, I remember thinking thirty minutes into our date, *Ben, you'd better kiss this girl tonight.* I was lovestruck by her and, naturally, I wanted to kiss her. Even though she told me she never kisses on the first date, I was going to change that. At the end of the night, after a really amazing time together, I leaned in and she leaned in. At the last second, I tricked her and gave her an Eskimo kiss—first, to keep her humble, and second, to play hard to get. I mean, she desperately wanted me to kiss her. She'll never admit that, but it's the truth. Physical affection has always played a big role in our relationship. We have never been shy about showing it, and I believe it's this kind of affection that has helped us have such a good relationship since day one.

"Always greet and depart with a kiss." More counsel from our marriage temple interview that rang true to us both. Neither of us will ever forget the time when we were dating and we had to take our separate cars back to Ben's house. We subconsciously left to make the drive without giving each other a kiss. No big deal, right? As soon as we both put our cars in drive, the whole drive there just felt *different*: a bad different. It felt like something was missing, and it was. We made a habit to *always* greet and depart with a kiss. But not just when you leave and return, just to show affection in general. That effort of actively thinking about it, then doing it, has *always* been a good idea. Every day. It may seem like a small detail that can be overlooked, but don't fall into this trap. Maybe a small departing kiss won't alter your life, but going a long time without them will.

This totally includes hand-holding too. And don't tell us your heart doesn't melt when you see an elderly couple holding hands in public. Their show of affection comes from years of building good relationship habits. However you show affection is fine, just make sure you show it every day. It could be playing with their hair while watching Netflix, giving them back scratches, or spooning. It includes footsie at the dinner table, even when you're eating at your in-laws'.

And we refuse to leave out the "love life." No blushing; we're serious. First, this is nothing to be embarrassed or ashamed about. It is sacred and created by God Himself.

There's a strengthening power that comes from intimacy, and it's important to have and keep that sacred connection between the two of you. That's how God wants it to be. Always keep your physical pull toward each other and act on it. Keeping your intimacy alive allows that sacred love and power to enter your relationship and will help bond you both together. Feel comfortable to talk about it, and always be open with each other. This should very much be a together thing and not a selfish or abused thing. It can't be one-sided or else it won't work the way it's meant to.

We've learned the importance of knowing and understanding each other's needs so that we can be sure to cater to them. Before we got married, we took an online test to see what our love languages were.[18] We recommend that everyone who is dating, or even those who are single, take this test. It's fun. According to a best-selling book, there are five different "languages" that we "speak" to give and receive love. It's stated that oftentimes you don't marry someone that speaks the same language as you, so it's important to see and understand your spouse's needs. We took the test as a joke initially, but it ended up really helping us understand how to best connect with each other, and how to be there in the ways we need.

Al: My love languages are service and words of affirmation. Which means, in order for me to feel the most loved, I need to be verbally told that I am loved, appreciated, or that I look pretty; I also react well to nice acts of kindness. When Ben does something like wash the dishes, or put away the clothes, that is when I think, *Wow, he really must love me because he did that.* Ben's love languages, on the other hand, are quality time and physical touch. The best way for him to feel loved is through one-on-one time with me, and any kind of physical touch (small things like holding hands). There are only five options in the test, and Ben and I didn't overlap. So, understanding our differences allowed us to better fulfill the other person's needs in small ways every day so that neither of us is left unsatisfied.

Balance

To lose balance sometimes for love is
part of living a balanced life.
—Elizabeth Gilbert, *Eat, Pray, Love*[19]

Al got a priesthood blessing that counseled her to never take her spouse for granted. Just because we live together and are around each other all the time, that doesn't mean it is okay to let our relationship with our spouse fall to the back burner. Since we heard that, it has been one of our top goals to use our time wisely and productively to strengthen our love for each other. We've learned to never put "things" before our spouse and to always seek ways to understand and show them that they are our priority. If we don't have time for love, we're doing something wrong.

Al: That advice has always been on the forefront of our minds, and I thought the advice was "cute." You know, making time for dating, affection, and stuff. And then my schedule started to get real crazy. My requests for more book signings were in high demand. I get about fifty requests to speak a day, not including all the other emails I get from my blog about everything you can think of. I fly and travel to speak in other states as frequently as I allow. And on top of being pulled in all these directions, I am working full time. All of these things are good things, and work is obviously necessary, but thinking, *If I don't make time for love, I'm doing something wrong,* is my driving force when accepting or declining opportunities. If I am not allowing enough time at home with my family, I'm doing it wrong.

Currently, I am completely booked for speaking events for an entire year out. Now, when I say I'm completely booked, I'm saying, I am absolutely action-packed and busy. But I absolutely have "free" time marked in my schedule for what should be our biggest priority—our family.

Mormon Channel came out with this beautifully honest video about falling out of love with a spouse. A beautiful love story unfolds in the beginning of the video, showing a couple falling in love and talking to each other every day on the phone, and with each conversation, they fall deeper in love with each other. After ten years of marriage and three kids, they both lose their jobs. He takes a new opportunity and then, for the third time, he leaves for eighteen months to go to a different country for work. The wife explains, "I felt like I was raising the family on my own. After a while, we were two complete strangers trying to make a family work. When he came back, it was the reality of living with somebody that, I honestly at the point, I didn't need anymore. . . . So, we decided to get divorced after thirteen years of marriage."[20] After their divorce, they decided to go to therapy together, for the sake of their kids. After only going a few times, the therapist tells them, "You guys are very stupid. Because these are things that you could have fixed before with help. . . . Maybe next time you guys can go on a date."[21]

In tears, the wife says, "So after thirteen years of being married, three children, a lot of pain, disagreements, loneliness, and a very painful divorce, we went on our first date again. He asked me out. We started smiling at each other again, and we started flirting, and he started sending silly text messages with emojis. . . . Even though that's not his personality, he did it."[22]

And she confessed, "I think I forgot the main part, *What am I doing to stay in love with him? What is he doing to stay in love with me?*"[23]

They recommitted to each other to make it work, to spend the time they needed *together*, and to make their relationship a priority. They continued to seek help. They continued to seek out spiritual things *together*. They were going to start praying together again. They started going to the temple together, and setting goals *together*. And they got remarried. And they remain happily married with their newfound priorities.[24]

Richard G. Scott shared:

> Once I learned an important lesson from my wife. I traveled extensively in my profession. I had been gone almost two weeks and returned home one Saturday morning. I had four hours before I needed to attend another meeting. I noticed that our little washing machine had broken down and my wife was washing the clothes by hand. I began to fix the machine.
>
> Jeanene came by and said, "Rich, what are you doing?"
>
> I said, "I'm repairing the washing machine so you don't have to do this by hand."
>
> She said, "No. Go play with the children."
>
> I said, "I can play with the children anytime. I want to help you."
>
> Then she said, "Richard, please go play with the children."
>
> When she spoke to me that authoritatively, I obeyed.
>
> I had a marvelous time with our children. We chased each other around and rolled in the fall leaves. Later I went to my meeting. I probably would have forgotten that experience were it not for the lesson that she wanted me to learn.

The next morning about 4:00 a.m., I was awakened as I felt two little arms around my neck, a kiss on the cheek, and these words whispered in my ear, which I will never forget: "Dad, I love you. You are my best friend."

If you are having that kind of experience in your family, you are having one of the supernal joys of life.[25]

LESSON FOUR

God's Will

Whatever God requires is right, no matter what it is,
although we may not see the reason thereof
till long after the events transpire.
—Joseph Smith[26]

God is in your corner. . . .
Everything will work for our good.
—Jeffrey R. Holland[27]

Before we met, we both were already committed to doing what Heavenly Father had in mind for us, so as a couple, it was never a question for us to continue to do so. It is, however, definitely interesting to follow the Spirit when it's not just yourself you are worrying about, but another person.

Al: Ever since my baptism, nothing has gone the way I had in mind. Things I really wanted and prayed for usually didn't come to pass. Things were unquestionably difficult and were usually hard to understand at the time. I have learned and relearned—over and over again—that even though I didn't understand why things didn't work out or why I was asked to do something extremely hard and against my own desires, that things always—every single time—turn out better than what I initially have in mind for myself. God's way, though it is usually more difficult, always leads to the greatest things that life has to offer.

It's hard when things don't go the way we have in mind, especially when they are righteous, good things that we want, like getting married. Sometimes, despite our best efforts and our faith, it just doesn't happen in our time frame, and that really stinks. But knowing that when we are trying, and knowing that God is in charge, we have to have faith that things will work how He wants them to.

Al: I was engaged to a boy that I didn't end up marrying. We had a date set in the temple and everything. He broke it off. He told me that he usually dates "really skinny brunettes," and that he "knew he could find someone much better." Brutal, right?

I had never been crushed so low in my entire life. My self-esteem was completely shattered. Even that is an understatement. I thought, *I'm not skinny enough or pretty enough. I am easily replaceable and, bluntly put, just not good enough.* How do you come back from hearing that from someone you were about to marry? But most of all, I had never been more spiritually confused in my entire life. Not because I wasn't with this guy, but because I thought I had been following the Spirit, so how could it not work out? What did I do wrong? Why was I being denied such a righteous desire? What was wrong with me?

I all of a sudden doubted my relationship with the Spirit—did I even really know Him? Had I been doing it wrong the whole time? Every day, no matter how hard I tried to be positive and strong, I'd still break down. Every day, I'd find myself screaming at and pleading with God that this whole thing would be over and that things could be different. And yet, it seemed that they weren't. I worked overtime every day, doing everything I could to try and get out of this spiritual and emotional slump that I couldn't seem to get out of no matter how many prayers I said. I longed for it to pass, and it didn't. I was mad, thinking that my faith and my God were failing me.

I learned an important principle during this time that has literally *changed my life*. I was tired of being upset. I was tired of being confused. I was tired of doubting myself and my efforts. So, I decided to stop.

Yep. I just decided to stop feeling that way. I was tired of it. I hated it. It wasn't healthy and it was bringing me, my spirit, and my progression down. It took a lot of prayer and help from God. But He is eager to show us the blessings and opportunities that He has to offer, so it wasn't as hard as I thought it would be once I really committed myself to it. It was help from God, and committing myself to actively look for the good that got me through it. I knew the good was there because God was there.

I learned a lot from that engagement not working out. One thing I learned was that, although I didn't get married then, the engagement was supposed to happen because it led me to a trial that provided vital lessons I needed to learn: lessons that I would be lost without knowing. Every bit of pain, confusion, discomfort, and loneliness wasn't for nothing; it was for the best and was 1,000 percent worth it. As hard as things were and continue to be, I am better. I am happy. I am progressing. And I am oh so blessed.

I learned that if we are trying, we will never be asked to go through things that wouldn't be for our good. Lessons and growth are there for us to become better. God is there. I learned time and time again that although nothing may go the way we want it to or pray for it to be, by following the Spirit it will always be profoundly better than we even knew was possible. All trials and course changes will lead us to better things and bigger blessings *every single time.* Things will be better than they were before the trial even came.

Sometimes we can't help but think how much easier it would be if things had gone the way we wanted them to go. But when we choose to remember God, little do we know what opportunities, people, growth, and blessings are right around the corner.

I learned that promised blessings never expire. Just because things haven't worked out yet, it doesn't mean they won't eventually.

Don't allow the passing of time to bring you doubt or cause you to settle for something less. Don't lose patience and miss out on what He has in store for you. And in the meantime, don't hold yourself back from learning and growing and experiencing other things. Just hold on, and don't lose confidence. Heavenly Father knows what's important to us and what we need.

Do not let time and trials dim your faith or diminish the truthfulness of His promises to you. Never lose confidence. His promises are so real. There are far, far better things ahead; I promise and God promises. That's what I love about Him; you will never be shortchanged from receiving the best blessings. Your prayers have been heard. But He has greater things in store for you. Accept the unexpected but profoundly greater path because it comes with the best blessings.

Stop living in the future, and enjoy today. Search for and learn to find joy in your trials, because surely there will be many. Love who you are and where you are. And never let a change of course take you away from the unchangeable truth that God is taking care of you. You may not have gone where you had in mind, but you will end up where you need to be, and will receive better blessings.

Following

Knowing that God's will for us is usually never what we initially had in mind, we made the decision that His will, in every situation, would be the most important, and that no matter what, we would work together to follow every prompting we received. Everyone reading this will probably know firsthand that it is not easy to follow through with something that you don't want to do or that you don't understand. As a companionship, we have had to learn and relearn that we have to overcome selfishness and pride in order to move forward together, and it takes a lot of communication and prayer. Sometimes, if one of us has received a prompting that was a little bold, we find that it can be difficult to bring it up to the other person for fear of how they will react or what they will think. We have come to just trust what the other has to say and really rely on our prayers together. And it's not just the prayers that are important; it's the listening afterward that we needed to focus on.

Ben: Discovering and following God's will isn't easy. It's a recurring thing that I keep relearning from the situations I've been in. I touched a little on this story in lesson two. When we were first married, one of the most difficult trials I had was not working. I made it more difficult because of my pride. Al was done with school and had a job. I looked for jobs and had plenty of interviews. I would get job offers, and oftentimes, I would accept them, only to get that feeling afterward that it wasn't right and God didn't want me to work at that time. Sometimes, I'd even go to an interview because of my desire to work, and God would tell me again that that's not what I was supposed to be doing, and I would turn down their offer during the interview. They would look at me like I was crazy! I've done that countless times. Who turns down a job nowadays, especially people my age? As a man, my pride and selfishness came out. Being married made it worse because I felt like I needed to be the bread-winner of our family, and that Al should be at home. I should be the one working, not her. I was thinking traditionally. I used to fear that it would affect our marriage because I wasn't working, or that I was letting someone down or that I would be judged.

I would tell Al all the time how bad I felt about it and how I felt like a bum. She would gently and lovingly rebuke me by saying, "All I want is for you to follow the Spirit." Or, "I just want you to be doing what God wants." And before I'd go to another interview, she'd remind me, "I will never be disappointed if you feel you need to decline it." I love that about her. She understands what God wants me to do and not do, and she supports that. I came to realize that He didn't want me to work a traditional nine-to-five, forty-hour-a-week job. It was super hard to learn that and was very humbling. I was counseled that I needed to just focus all my efforts on my education. It wasn't time for me to work yet, and the right job would come and be prepared for me. How confusing and upsetting it was to hear that over and over again. Eventually, I swallowed my pride and focused on school.

After a year of marriage and while I was attending LDS Business College, I felt that I should start a business. After praying and talking with Al on one of our nightly walks, I pursued this endeavor. I could work from home, do school, and be with our daughter, Gracie. It was a win-win. I started a company, and it became successful—in my opinion. It kept me busy and it was a lot of fun. This was the kind of job that God wanted me to have because it gave me the flexibility and freedom to do the things I needed to do. I ran that company for two years until I was prompted to do something else.

Not working, and dealing with the internal struggle I had when I accepted the path that God wanted for me, was definitely one of the most humbling and ongoing experiences I have ever dealt with in my life. Not only is following God's will sometimes hard, but it may not even make sense. But the blessings do come, and I have seen those blessings with my education, my wife, and my two kiddos. No matter how hard following God's will may seem, just know that you are in His hands, and that is the best place to be.

Trusting God means embracing the unexpected and knowing who is guiding us. It's knowing that we'd be giving up something good for something better. God's will is not knowing how things will work out, but just knowing that they will.

Al: I was very adamant that we would wait at least a year or two after being married before we would ever consider having kids. It was something that I felt so strongly about and my stubborn New Yorker kicked into full gear and I was positive I wouldn't budge on it. Ben and I had other plans; we wanted to travel and just enjoy each other one-on-one. After only a month of being married, Ben came to me and said that he thought we should have a baby. I literally laughed in his face and asked if he was joking. He wasn't. I'm not sure what my face did exactly, but it felt new and completely unnatural because of how surprised I was. I tried to forget that he had even mentioned it to me, but the thought kept creeping back into my head. I was actually too afraid to ask God in prayer if that was something we needed to do because I knew if I got an answer I would have to act on it and I didn't want to act on this one.

I have come to learn that for me, those reoccurring thoughts are usually already a sure sign that it's God's will because the Spirit often speaks to me in reoccurring thoughts. I was stubborn and selfish, but we took it to the temple. Sure enough, we both felt strongly that we should have a child together. We acted on it. We got pregnant. And once it was confirmed to me that it was right and that it was God's will for us, comfort immediately followed; it was the most exciting time of our life. Once we know how much God loves us and how He always wants to give us the best that He's created, and once we know that God knows us better than we know ourselves and that He knows our whole lives on earth, following a prompting from Him becomes exciting! I was so pumped and anxious to see it all unfold. And now, we've just had our second baby. But we also can't imagine having either of our kids at different times than when they came. God's timing truly is best. I couldn't imagine our life together without them, and it kills me to think that I almost didn't listen and follow through. The easiest way to get closer to your spouse is to follow through with anything hard or new together as a team. There is something about overcoming and conquering things together that brings a strong connection and closeness that is hard to break.

> If I did only what I wanted to do, I would not be obedient to the Creator. Sometimes He wants us to do certain things that we may not feel like doing. When it comes to what God asks of us, we need more than good intentions—we need to follow through fully.
> —John Wooden[28]

Sometimes God's will for us comes at times when we least expect it or when we think it may be inconvenient. Ben's dad recently told us a story that he heard from a speaker in sacrament meeting one Sunday. This young family was living in Texas. The husband had a great career, and they had just built their dream home. They had designed it their way, and even had a full-size soccer field in their backyard because they loved soccer. Six months after living in their dream home, the husband got called in for a meeting at work. His boss had discovered that he spoke fluent Japanese and told him that they wanted to promote him and relocate him and his family to Japan. He and his wife were shocked. What timing, right? They *just* built their dream home! Their kids *loved* it there. He went to Japan to get a feel for things there and to give it a chance, but he became *really* sick and had to be sent home. He hadn't wanted to move there to begin with, but after becoming so ill and having to leave, he really didn't want to bring his family there. After their nightly prayer together as a couple, they were surprised because they both felt prompted that God wanted them to leave their dream home and move to Japan.

So, they did. And that was that. They ended up living in Japan for fifteen years and loved it there. The speaker shared how the decision to leave their dream home and move to Japan brought some of the biggest blessings they have ever received as a family. God's will for them may have come at an inconvenient time, but they knew that doing what He wanted was more important than what they wanted.

Though it doesn't come close to the scale of that story, there was a time when we desperately wanted to buy a home. In fact, we still do. Gracie was a newborn, and we had two dogs. We felt like it was finally time. On Christmas Eve morning, we met with our friend who is a mortgage lender, and we got approved to buy a home that same day. We were beyond excited! We spent *a lot* of time in January looking at lots of different homes and determining what we really wanted, but the search was tough. Despite our desires and our efforts, toward the end of January, Ben mentioned that he felt that we shouldn't buy a home yet and should instead move to Arizona.

Ben: Arizona came as a huge surprise. It really was a lightning-style prompting. It came fast and it was clear. Al flat out told me, "No! We're buying a house. That's what we wanted to do. We are not moving to Arizona." I persisted all week that Arizona was the correct move to make. We decided to go to the temple together to hopefully get on the same page. And it wasn't until we went to the Lord's house together that Al got her answer that Arizona was right. Once we both knew that it was His will, we never looked back.

God's will came to us at the right time. We felt that buying a home was the right choice, so we pursued it, but God let us know that He had something else in mind. It should come as no surprise that moving to Arizona was one of the best decisions we have ever made; we are *still* living in some of the blessings that decision gave us. No matter how random or how unwanted an idea may seem at first, don't dismiss new ideas that come to either of you; *explore them* with God.

There's no doubt that God's will can sometimes put you in a scary situation or in a circumstance that doesn't fully make sense. But Heavenly Father will never ask us to do something that isn't for our absolute best.

We often think back to a simple response that President Dieter F. Uchtdorf mentioned in one of his general conference talks. In reference to following God's will, he says, "I think God knows something we don't—things that are beyond our capacity to comprehend!"[29]

He goes on to say,

Our Father in Heaven is an eternal being whose experience, wisdom, and intelligence are infinitely greater than ours. Not only that, but He is also eternally loving, compassionate, and focused on one blessed goal: to bring to pass our immortality and eternal life.

In other words, He not only *knows* what is best for you; He also anxiously *wants you to choose* what is best for you.

If you believe this in your hearts—if you truly believe the great mission of our Heavenly Father is to exalt and glorify His children and that He knows best how to do it—doesn't it make sense to embrace and follow His commandments, even the ones that appear difficult?[30]

Recognizing

God will always come through. He will show us the right path. He knows that some decisions are big decisions, and He wants us to pray to Him and trust and believe in the Holy Ghost's ability to help us make the right choice together. He will tell us the way, and we are asked to just give God the chance to show us the greater things that He has in store for us here. So what do we do if we can't recognize what He wants us to do?

Ben: When we were living in Coolidge, Arizona, I felt torn mentally and spiritually about making a decision that was going to affect our family. There were two possibilities, but both of them felt right, and I felt confused because they both seemed right. I thought that one had to outweigh the other. I had a trusted friend in Coolidge that I called and asked to come over to our house and give me some counsel and a blessing. I was told something surprising in that blessing. I was told that sometimes both choices are good and right choices. I was told that Heavenly Father wanted me to decide so that I could learn from my decisions. I was obviously surprised to hear that, but it changed my way of thinking. Knowing that both choices I had in mind were good and right, but that Heavenly Father was giving me the opportunity to decide, made a difference. No matter what I chose, I knew that I was doing the right thing because I was doing what God wanted me to do. And it helped to know that He was aware of me.

But what about the other times when that isn't the case? Some of you may be asking yourself, *Yeah, I totally want to do God's will too, but how do I know what that is?* How can we discern between our thoughts and the Spirit?

Al: I know that I don't want something if God doesn't want it for me. Yet how many prayers have I spent asking Heavenly Father to just tell me what He wants me to do so I can do it, and then still felt like I was going in circles? Do you know how much time I've spent wasting and waiting and worrying—feeling stuck because I felt like I couldn't understand a clear answer about what to do? And the more time I spent thinking about one decision over the other—battling with thoughts and fears and blessings for each choice—the more confused I became and the harder it got.

God doesn't always tell us what is right. But He has promised that He will always tell us what is *not* right.

We were living in Arizona when I lost my job. We were living off of our savings, and we both tried desperately for seven months to find any kind of work. Even in our desperate situation, nothing worked out. Our savings account was obviously dwindling to nothing at this point when I randomly got a call from Church headquarters in Utah; they were offering me a job that paid almost double what I had been making at my previous job. A miracle, right? Well, kind of. Even in our desperate situation and during the longest trial we've ever had together, I didn't want it. I was willing to have us live on the street before leaving Arizona. We wanted to buy a house there and stay there for the rest of our lives. Life had never seemed better to me than when we were in that state. And even when we were unemployed, my trials seemed to not be as hard because I could walk outside and see the palm trees and feel the warm breeze that was always there. I was nervous to tell Ben that I didn't want to take the only opportunity that could rescue us from our financial devastation. Plus, at the time, I was pregnant with our second child. I can imagine that he was a little mad when I told him, but he responded, "If that's how you really feel." Well, it technically was, but I knew what he was referring to, and that was a spiritual "feel," which I didn't have.

I didn't even ask God, actually. I didn't want to. Here was the perfect job opportunity back in Utah, and I had to decide by that night. I was on a deadline to get back to them, and I didn't have time to go back and forth between my feelings and the Spirit—asking God yes-or-no questions and struggling to figure out if they were my feelings or His. A trick I have learned when figuring out God's will, is to sometimes not ask it as a yes-or-no, right-or-not question. It is telling Him what you decided and asking if it's wrong.

I have learned, the long and hard way, that God doesn't always tell us what is right. But He always tells us what is wrong. He has to; it's His promise to us if we turn to Him and listen. So, I did that. I told God I wasn't going to take it and I told Him why. Then I told him that if it was wrong, He would have to tell me before 9 a.m. when I was going to send my response back to the Church, declining their offer. That was that. But then I woke up. I woke up at 5 a.m. and I couldn't sleep for the life of me. My heart was beating out of my chest, my body was tingly, and my mind and my soul absolutely knew—without a doubt—that I needed to take that job. And I did.

And I cried. A lot. But our trial ended and we aren't just "getting by." Because we followed His will, we have thrived and flourished in ways that we couldn't have imagined on our own.

> Mine eyes are upon you, and the heavens and the earth are in mine hands, and the riches of eternity are mine to give.
>
> Ye endeavored to believe that ye should receive the blessing which was offered unto you; but behold, verily I say unto you there were fears in your hearts, and verily this is the reason that ye did not receive. (D&C 67:2–3)

Choose faith over fear, and you will see your journey as a companionship unfold before your eyes. You will experience the greatest blessings that God has in store for you, greater than you even knew were available.

Have joy where you are. Enjoy where you are led. Enjoy the unknown. Enjoy and get excited about those bold promptings, knowing that they are handpicked by God: a perfect God who makes no mistakes.

We have learned that by delaying a prompting, we are only delaying the most rewarding blessings that we didn't even know existed. Comfort will always come. Help and guidance and open doors will always present themselves. Forget not whose hands we're in. Fear not. In scripture, all of the promises and blessings that we are trying so hard to receive, are all written in the past tense: "Prepar*ed*." Those promises and blessings are already there! Heavenly Father has already spent the time, the love, and the effort into creating the best for us. And we can have it, not just later in the eternities, but here. All we have to do is keep going, keep trusting, and keep choosing God over our narrow, prideful ideas of how our life should go. All we have to do is continue. Continue in God. Continue opening up to each other about our ideas, even if they are unwanted, hard, or crazy. Continue to seek the Lord together. Continue to go to the temple—a place where the adversary is not allowed in, not even in our thoughts. Continue to listen to recurring thoughts. And continue to allow God to show us how great He really is.

Lesson Five

Do Hard Things Together

God loves us. He is good. He is our Father and He
expects us to pray and trust and be believing and not
give up and not panic and not retreat . . . when
something doesn't seem to be going just right.
—Elder Jeffrey R. Holland[31]

If we magnified blessings as much as we magnify
disappointments, we would all be much happier.
—John Wooden[32]

Ben: Just two weeks into our very new dating relationship, Al texted me early in the morning from work, saying she was having some really bad pain in her side. She thought it would go away with medicine, and we both didn't think much of it at first. But it got worse. And when she went a long time without texting me back, I couldn't stop worrying about her. I eventually received a call from her boss saying he had rushed her to the ER. Al's appendix had burst! And she was being taken in for emergency surgery. I was freaking out. I hurried and bolted down I-15 to the hospital. By the time I got there, Al was already out of surgery and was pretty drugged. At the time, Al lived in a two-bedroom home by herself with her dog Lucas. After the surgery, she couldn't move around well at all, and wouldn't be able to for several days. She didn't have anyone to help take care of her during her recovery. So I made her stay at my parents' house so I could help her.

Plus, this was a win for me because I could have her all to myself and see her all day. Her recovery was fun; she was loopy, which made it all the merrier. But only two weeks into us knowing each other, this was a great opportunity for us to really spend time together, serve one another, and interact with each other when one of us wasn't at our best. Al and I learned early on to embrace the hard things together and to not shy away from them. We learned from this experience to take on those hard times together and to look for opportunities to grow, learn, serve, and come together. Because we look for those things when faced with hard situations, our difficult times can become cherished times together.

Hard times will be there, but doing them together as a team makes them easier to handle. Now, not every dating relationship needs a surgery story. But no matter how difficult a situation may be, do it together. Show love and be there for one another.

Doing hard things together as a team can mean tons of things: buying a house, deciding where to live, going to school, having kids, getting jobs. The list goes on. Any big decision or hard choice that you can think of is included here and should never be made by one spouse alone. Every decision, big or small, affects *both of you*, and should be worked on and decided by *both of you*. No surprise decisions should be told to your spouse without them having input in the decision process: "Honey, I am moving all of us to Denver next month for a new job opportunity I accepted." If one of you receives revelation or an idea, you both need to talk it out and seek counsel and confirmation together as a team before anything is confirmed. Get on the same page. Work it out. Include your spouse in the decision process because this is very much their life too; they have every right to have a say in every matter. Talk about the pros and cons of these decisions. Together, seek the Lord and His will through your prayers and temple attendance. Because decisions affect *everyone* in your family, not just yourself, everyone's input should be considered. A sure way to disrupt trust between the two of you is acting like their feelings and input are not valid. *They are always valid.*

The strength of companionship is laced throughout all scripture. But here's one that we really like:

> Alma labored much in the spirit, wrestling with God in mighty prayer, that he would pour out his spirit upon the people who were in the city [Ammonihah]. . . .
>
> Nevertheless, they hardened their hearts . . .
>
> And withstood all his words, and reviled him, and spit upon him, and caused that he should be cast out of their city. (Alma 8:10–11, 13)

The humiliation and persecution that Alma faced in that moment had to be one of the most difficult times in his life. In contrast, just before this, in the city of Melek, Alma had so much success. Alma suffered greatly, "being weighed down with sorrow, wading through much tribulation and anguish of soul" (Alma 8:14). He was giving up on the people of Ammonihah and was on his way to a different city, Could you blame him? But then an angel of the Lord appeared to him and comforted Alma, saying, "Blessed art thou, Alma; therefore, lift up thy head and rejoice" (Alma 8:15). The angel urged Alma to not give up, but to keep trying, and to *go back* to Ammonihah and to those same people. Alma, being the obedient prophet that he was, returned "speedily" to the land of Ammonihah (see Alma 8:18).

On his way back, he met Amulek—someone that the Lord prepared to be a companion for him. Amulek would become one of Alma's closest friends. He would become someone who would suffer *with him*, be beaten with him, and be spit upon with him, and they would see many trials *together*. They spent many days together at Amulek's home before Alma returned to that same vile city that had rejected him. But this time, with Amulek, and after suffering so much, they saw much success together.

Heavenly Father cares about what we go through, and He will always provide a way for us to get through it. No matter what we face in life, God will help us through it. Spencer W. Kimball taught this concept when he said, "God does notice us, and he watches over us. But it is usually through another person that he meets our needs."[33] For Alma, He provided a companion—someone to help him preach the gospel.

God provides a spouse for us—someone who will be there for us and help us in our times of struggle and need. Once we are married, our individual trials should not be so individual anymore. We have to be able to work together as a team, and "my" trials are now "our" trials. We have to be willing to be open and actively help them with whatever it is they are going through. Whatever they are going through, we are going through it with them together. We have learned that simply asking what we can do to help is not good enough. We must actively seek out and follow through. We need to overcome our pride or selfishness to allow our partner to help us. As we allow them into our trials, it will strengthen us personally and in our marriage. Hard things in life will not seem as hard when they are done together. And it's hardly a coincidence at all when we realize that our spouse *just happens* to be strong on our weak days, and vice versa.

Al: My first pregnancy was the longest trial I have had to go through, and yes, I do view it as a trial. I hated it. I hated almost everything about it. Yes, it was worth it, and yes, I am grateful that I was even able to have gone through it, but you know what, that doesn't take away from the fact that sometimes it was unbearably hard. It was a struggle throughout all of it and I hated that. Not only did I not feel like myself, but I couldn't seem to do anything about it because of how sick I was. I hated how something that I was going through affected Ben's life so much, and when I thought about that it would make things even worse.

I would get in terrible moods because I felt so bad that Ben and I had to cancel plans with our friends because I was too tired, or that we had to leave activities early because I felt so nauseated. And I felt bad that we couldn't even enjoy church in the chapel; we had to sit in the foyer where I wouldn't sweat like a pig. I felt absolutely horrible that I was the reason that we had to stop working in the temple because I literally passed out on top of a patron during an ordinance! (I am still convinced that I forever traumatized that poor girl whose lap I face-planted into.) It wasn't just me going through this; he was too. I felt like I was bringing him down and that I would be responsible for him ever feeling unhappy, if he ever did feel that way. I was afraid his love for me would weaken because I wasn't the happy and strong girl that he fell in love with. I felt like I was a giant burden—plain and simple—and he shouldn't have to deal with that.

Not once did Ben ever get upset by anything we couldn't do. Not once was blame ever pointed toward me. Not once did he ever sigh or roll his eyes, and not once did I ever feel like I was alone in this. He was constantly going out and looking online to research home remedies to try and help me. He was constantly surprising me with things that I was too stubborn to get on my own. He knew I couldn't get comfortable enough during the night to fall asleep, so he came home one night and surprised me with a pregnancy pillow that was an absolute lifesaver. He would already have the car stocked with snacks to help with my nausea before it ever kicked in. We are front-row sitters in sacrament meeting, and I felt guilty to be the one responsible for changing that, but he was the one to insist on sitting in the foyer where the AC was better, so I wouldn't pass out again. Without me saying anything, he would pick up on the small things I would do that showed my discomfort and would go out to Redbox and come back and surprise me with a new movie for the night so I could relax. His actions of service and patience never wore thin, and it always surprised me.

I was surprised at how often I could laugh when I was having the most miserable day, and I was surprised at how much our love grew even stronger during the times when I felt that it would have the complete opposite effect. I found that we work better as a team than we ever did or could on our own, and the hard things in life are easier when we do them together. I was asked a question once, "What's the one thing that brings you the most joy?" And I thought, *Easy, my husband.* Then, *Wait. No, God. Wait.* And as I was thinking much deeper than I think was intended for this question, I realized how perfectly Heavenly Father has blessed me with Ben, and how He uses him every day, a million times a day, to help and bless me and answer my prayers. I even asked Ben once, "Why are you still here? How can you do this every day?" He responded, "I promised Heavenly Father I'd take care of you." I'm incredibly grateful for my husband—for his strengths and passions, and his humor and patience in my life. But I'm mostly grateful for his love and the joy that he has for God, which truly makes what we have incredible.

Ben: When we found out we were pregnant with Gracie, I was on the phone with Al's mom when Al came out of the bathroom with the results. I didn't even need to see the test to know the outcome. She was crying with this huge smile on her face, and I just hung up the phone. This was one of the most special moments we had ever shared together; we couldn't have been more excited! But this pregnancy also brought a lot of hard times with it. Al didn't have the easiest pregnancy; it was very difficult for her. I always knew that pregnancy was tough, but I had no idea it was going to be like how it was for her. It was tough seeing her get sick every day, and coming home early from work because of it, or not even being able to be in the car for ten minutes without getting carsick. I hated seeing my wife struggle so much and feel so low with her self-esteem. She would worry too much about me and how I was doing with all this. But I never had any negative feelings toward her, and I never wondered, "Where is my wife?" I didn't care that she went to bed at 7 p.m. every night.

I just knew that I wanted to try to be there for her and try to help her in any way that I could. I made it my absolute goal to go through every little bit of this experience with her. I wished I could have taken her pain away, so that way she could have a break, but realizing that I couldn't do that, I made an effort to ease her burdens instead. I'm pretty weird and random, so I would try to do silly things to make her laugh. I would fast all the time for her, and most importantly, I would show and give her love.

I learned that pregnancy isn't just for the woman; the men are involved and have a big role too. We obviously can't take away the suffering, but we can make each day for them a little better and more fun. And that rule goes for any trial. I love my wife, and after seeing her go through that, she became my hero. It wasn't easy, but it taught me a deeper feeling of love and support. I had never wept in my life until Gracie was born. I'm grateful every day to Al for giving me my two treasures: Gracie and Christian.

Our closest married-couple friends recently went through something very difficult in their marriage. Dave and Liz (names changed) are literally the "perfect match," and were living a very normal newlywed life together. Only a few years into their marriage, one of Liz's past habits became a struggle again. As a young teenager, she had struggled with an eating disorder, and now it had returned. At first, it started as some quirks that she thought she could control, but then the downward spiral started and it became worse. Dave and Liz started to not be able to leave the house. She had to quit her job, and they had to cancel most of their plans because she felt ill all the time.

Though this was a past struggle of hers, this was new information for her husband. Obviously, he was concerned and aware of the seriousness of it, and he quickly found a counselor that they both felt good about.

As she was reliving this pain, she opened up to her counselor and then her husband about these deep hidden secrets that caused her to relapse and cope with her eating disorder just like when she was a teenager. Except this time, it was worse.

She became so unhealthy and sick that she was almost unrecognizable. She became too frail to even sit up, so she would spend her days lying in her bed, not moving. One particularly bad night, Dave rushed Liz to the ER and the doctors told him that if he would have waited a little longer, Liz may have died. She was admitted full time to a rehab center for six months, forcing them to be separate from each other.

Through all of this, even with their time apart, we saw Dave fully embrace and accept everything from the start. We saw him weep with her. We saw him hurt right there with her. We saw him love deeper. We saw him consistently making sure that she got the help she needed, and recognizing the times when he knew it couldn't come from him, but had to come from professionals. We saw that even in his dark and tiring times, his countenance shone even brighter than before as he sought after the Lord with all the energy he had. We saw him sacrifice so much. And we saw them both cry *together*. We saw them pull *closer*. We saw him on the phone with her while she was in rehab, praying together. We saw her years of built-up fears, embarrassment, guilt, and shame fade as she opened up to him and he embraced and accepted her right from the start. We saw her comforted in their darkest times. We saw her progress and heal. And from a distance, we saw the two of them strengthen together, fall even deeper in love, become even more closely connected, and draw closer to the Lord.

Here's the thing about hard times—*they're hard*. But what makes them harder is when you feel like you're alone in them. Do the hard things *together*. Actively look for ways to draw closer to each other. Always look for ways to serve and lighten their load. Always embrace them and express love and gratitude. And always turn to God for inspiration on how to help or answer their prayers. Because even if it's not "*you*" that is struggling, our "I's" are always "We's."

After man was created, God looked upon the earth, and the earth was not finished until Eve was then created for Adam. It is intended for us—for more reasons then we will fully be able to comprehend on this earth—to have a companion. It is intended for us to have that help, support, and love. We've come to realize that being married and handling challenging situations and decisions together makes them a lot easier. Even when we feel like we are going through something individually or alone, having someone along with you, supporting you always and seeking out ways to comfort and lift any part of your burden, means you can conquer almost anything. Life is hard and that will not change, but there's nothing you can't do if you do it together.

Lesson Six

God First, Bro

I knew that he [her husband, Gordon B. Hinckley] loved me
and that he would always be good to me. But I also knew that
I would never come first with him and that was okay. I knew
[he] was going to devote his life to the Lord. And I couldn't
think of anyone I'd rather have him devoted to.
—Marjorie Pay Hinckley[34]

When we put God first, all other things fall into
their proper place or drop out of our lives.
—Ezra Taft Benson[35]

Triangle

Thou shalt love the Lord thy God with all thy heart, and with all thy soul, and with all thy mind, and with all thy strength: this is the first commandment. (Mark 12:30)

When we are married, our relationship should work like a triangle; God is the top point, and the bottom two points are you and your spouse. When you are both moving closer toward God, you find yourselves closer to each other too. The most important relationship we can ever have is our relationship with God. We need to make a continuous effort to put Heavenly Father at the forefront of our lives in all circumstances. This relationship with Him is never to be taken for granted or forgotten; this is what will help all of our other relationships in life. We are to open up to Him and talk to Him just as we would with our closest friend. We cannot limit our time with Heavenly Father to only when it is convenient, when we need something from Him, or when it's a Sunday. We are to turn to Him with all of our problems, decisions, and needs.

It is only through Him that we receive the best blessings to ever be offered in this world and the world to come— blessings that are greater than we even knew existed, and greater than we even knew were available for us to receive. Not just in the eternities, but here, daily. "Every good gift and every perfect gift is from above, and cometh down from the Father of lights" (James 1:17).

It is because of God and through Christ that we are able to change and become better. We can only become our best selves by turning to Them, making time for Them, using our own efforts to learn of Them, and strengthening our relationship with Them. Only with Their help can we overcome and conquer absolutely everything.

In the scriptures, there is a recurring phrase spoken by Jesus Christ. He tells us and beckons us to come unto Him. "Come unto me" is all over in the scriptures because Christ wants us to come to Him. He wants us to come home and lay all of our troubles, worries, and burdens on Him. We cannot do it alone, and we're not here on earth to do it alone; we must come unto Christ and follow Him. It's the same with our marriages. If we want to be the best husband or wife that we can be, we do that by coming unto the Lord. If your marriage is having trials or hardships, come unto the Lord; He makes "weak things become strong" (see Ether 12:27). He can make us better and stronger, which, in turn, makes our marriages stronger. Seeking Christ—daily and often—is what will lead all of us to the full potential we are capable of in this life.

That's why Heavenly Father is at the top of the triangle; He comes to help us when we reach up to Him and do our part. But it's not just love that will hold up the foundation of our marriage on the tough days and through our times of being tested; we have to have a relationship with our Father in Heaven, both individually and collectively, to help our marriage grow and blossom.

Ben: The triangle has been a symbol, and even a logo, of how we want to structure our marriage. It has been great to have a wife who is awesome about doing spiritual things. She is such an example to me about striving to seek and use the gospel daily. Her own personal connection with God is key when I'm having a tough day or going through trials, because she is the one who helps me get through those rough times with her encouragement and spiritual strength. The triangle has reminded us of how important it is to keep God at the head of our marriage; if we really want to accomplish the goals and desires that we have set for our lives, it is only possible to do so by aligning our will with God's will. It isn't easy; we have our share of arguments and disagreements where we don't see eye to eye, and there are many times when we both let our pride come before the Spirit. But during those times when we actively focus on the triangle (Heavenly Father), we are refocused and helped, and those disagreements are settled. Giving up when things are hard or when things don't go our way or giving up on each other isn't an option, nor should it ever be.

Soul Food

The reality is, we have a spiritual being living *within* us, and we thrive when we feed it. We are our best when we are taking the time we deserve, *and need*, to improve our soul. Because if we are not taking care of ourselves, how can we help and be there for others? This headline is pretty straightforward, but oh so important. If things feel *off*, whether with yourself or in your marriage, take time to make a checklist of things that you can be doing for yourself to possibly fix that.

Have you allowed time for yourself? Have you fed your soul lately? Are you seeking personal revelation? Are you taking time to listen and converse with the Holy Ghost? Are you going to the temple? Are you aware and following through with daily repentance? Are you moving closer to God? Because, like a triangle, when we are moving closer to God, we are moving closer to our spouse.

We have learned that if we argue or if we are going through a rough patch, or we catch each other acting *off*, we sit and talk to each other; we ask how well we are doing with seeking Heavenly Father and Christ. We've noticed that some of the troubles in our marriage were made worse when we weren't doing spiritual things that day, or during the past few days, to make us better for each other when hard times come. Some troubles only come as a result when we slack spiritually for whatever reason. Set goals to become better spiritually and to seek God; the closer you are to God, the closer you will be with your spouse.

Al: I work full time, and I have built a routine around my schedule. Every Monday–Friday, I wake up at 6:00 a.m.; I pray for help and energy, and then I work out; I shower; I pray again for help with my scripture study; I get ready for work; I pray with Ben before I leave the house (even when he's still asleep); I go to work, and on my way home, I always pray out loud in the car. And when I'm not speaking or traveling, I am home spending time with Ben and our kids. Some days I don't have that prayer on my way home, for whatever reason. Those nights just happen to be the nights that I'm not as pleasant, proactive, or awake as I usually am. I find myself getting bugged about stupid stuff that I wouldn't normally care about, or I feel lazy. Almost every single time I notice myself acting this way, I immediately have the thought, "Oh shoot, I didn't say my prayer for the Spirit to help me!"

We become a better spouse and parent when we make time to take care of ourselves and our soul. We do that by giving God the time He deserves, and the time our spirit needs to thrive. Change and growth is a gift from, and because of, God. So naturally, we can't do those things without Him. Let's help each other out and hold each other accountable to make sure we are doing those things that we need. Just like we mentioned before in our communication chapter, tell each other your goals. Be open. Tell each other what you want and need to do better with. And help each other. Hold each other accountable. Set time apart for each other.

We're not saying that we know all things, but we are saying that God does. We are saying that God blesses us when we turn to him and do as He would have us do. Blessings, help, and counsel come when we are faithful and when we seek the Lord. Our challenges will not always be removed, but we will always receive the strength and guidance to be able to handle what we are going through. What our Father in Heaven can do for us is endless, but He can't do anything for us if we don't turn to Him in trust.

Make the Temple Your Centerpiece

Al was told in a priesthood blessing, right when we got married, that the temple should be our centerpiece. A centerpiece is pretty self-explanatory: it is placed in the center and everything else is placed and works around it. In that same blessing, we were told that we should have a picture of a temple in every room of our house, even the bathrooms, to help us be mindful of the temple when we weren't inside its walls. With the help of Deseret Book and pass-along cards, we listened.

We are to seek the Lord with our spouse, and if we are looking for the Lord, we will find Him in His house. (Unintentional rhyme—nice!) Going to the temple together was established the very first day we met; our first date was literally at the temple. Since the day we met, we made it a goal to go weekly, even before we were engaged. The temple was important to both of us, and it was even more important that we established it as the centerpiece of our relationship together. We grew spiritually together. We set good habits right off the bat. We were attracted to each other spiritually. We fed our souls. We learned how to receive revelation together in the temple. We most definitely don't recommend your first dates be to the temple per se, but having that desire and goal to build together early is the perfect way to start off and continue strong spiritual habits. There is a real power that comes from a husband and wife, or an engaged couple, participating in the Lord's holiest ordinances.

While dating, if you can, go as often as you can to the temple together, even if you aren't endowed yet. Do baptisms. It's important to set good, spiritual habits as early as you can. And as you're planning your wedding, focus on the sealing. Not just while you're being sealed, but while *planning* your wedding. When we stay focused on the most important thing—our covenants—then what goes into planning will usually be things that matter, and we will avoid getting frustrated over menial things, like a soft yellow versus an eggshell yellow. Yes, plan your reception. Yes, spend time getting a dress or a tux you feel comfortable in. But if we are only planning and preparing for tangible things, we'll be missing the point. Prepare for your sealing just like you are preparing for your reception. Spiritually prepare for going to the temple. Some of you may not have been endowed yet, so start going to temple prep classes. Increase your testimony. The stronger your testimony is, the more ready you'll be for making more covenants; you'll be more understanding, accepting, and receptive to spiritual things and the things of God, simple as that.

Getting sealed is the last ordinance there is, which says a lot about how important the family is to God. We recommend getting endowed as early as you are allowed, which we think is two weeks before your sealing date, so you can really focus on the ordinances and covenants without the whirlwind of everything that goes into a wedding. Try to go as often as you can before your wedding day, so that you can better understand what promises you made, and so that you can build that experience, relationship, and habit with your soon-to-be spouse. Do sealings with your soon-to-be spouse, with temple names, before your own sealing. Often times, the first time people do a sealing is when it is their own, and 99 percent don't remember what was said. Most of us love the idea of "forever families" because it sounds romantic. But it's not just there to be cute. It's essential. We aren't just sealed to our spouse; we're sealed to Christ. These promises are absolutely incredible, and are the perfect way to know what you and your spouse will receive and have together as a companionship. If you can't do sealings before your own for whatever reason, go back as soon as you are back from your honeymoon, if not before or during it.

Joseph Smith taught that we need the temple more than we need anything else. It is there that we learn more of God and more of ourselves. It is where we learn our full purpose and potential, where we learn about our promises from God and where we make promises with Him in return. It's where we receive answers to our prayers and the strength to continue. It is there that our love for God and Christ strengthens, and it is there that our love for our spouse and family grows.

All of our major decisions and revelations have come from service in His house. The decision to not buy a house in Provo came in the Jordan River Utah Temple; the decision to move to Arizona came in the Salt Lake Temple; the decision to get married came in the Oquirrh Mountain Utah Temple. The decision to have both of our kids, what job we should or shouldn't take, what Ben should go to school for—everything came while we were in the temple.

The house of the Lord is exactly that—His house. He dwells, walks, and returns often within those sacred walls. The adversary is not allowed, not even in the waiting room. Satan cannot have any influence on your thoughts as you enter into the Lord's home. You'll solve problems and find answers better and more quickly in the house of the Lord than anywhere else. Strength in all aspects of our lives—spiritual, mental, and physical—comes from our attendance there. Sheri Dew once said, "*Every* worthy adult may go to the temple, from which he or she emerges surrounded and protected by God's power,"[36] and we *need* that power. Go often, go together, and go *prepared* and pondering. How much we learn and receive in the temple depends upon our mind-set and preparedness going in.

Ben: I have never met anyone who loves the temple more than my wife does. She was previously endowed before we met, and she had a routine of going every week on top of working every Saturday night in the Provo Utah Temple as an ordinance worker. Her love for the temple and her desire to attend frequently has rubbed off on me from her example and passion. When we got married, the first thing we said to our new bishop was that we wanted to work in the temple, and we did! We worked the Saturday afternoon shift at the Jordan River Utah Temple; it was so much fun to be there together and to see each other working. We grew together during that time, and we understood more about the temple and its importance. We would look forward to Saturdays because of our duties there. I can tell you that there is nothing like working at heaven on earth and seeing the Spirit work on tons of people a day. If you are able to, and your schedule allows it, totally work in the temple together. Being there together and helping the Lord's work move forward is special, and there's nothing like it! I would encourage you to prayerfully think about it; it's a deeply sacred experience that will bring you both together.

Temple work brings so much resistance because it is the source of so much spiritual power. For those that live close to a temple, they usually have the mind-set of, "Well, if I don't make it this week, there's always next week," and that is how the adversary gets to us. The knowledge that the temple isn't going anywhere allows other things to come before our attendance and then procrastination sweeps in. It becomes easy to take for granted what the temple truly is, and what comes from going there and going often. To make and keep the temple as your centerpiece, sit down with your spouse and plan for it. Mark on your calendar what days you will go and keep them there; plan for it and plan around it. Do not make excuses.

When we were pregnant, almost everyone told us, "Well, when that baby comes you won't be able to go to the temple anymore," and, "Say your goodbyes now because that'll end when you're parents." We even heard sad stories of, "Since our baby was born, it has been a few years since we have been back to the temple, and it's only gotten harder." We had never been parents before, so we couldn't say how life would be with a newborn and a growing child, but we were determined to keep the temple at the core of our marriage. We have learned to not let what other people say influence us when it comes to what it is we can and cannot do. Don't let other people freak you out. You really can do whatever it is that you want to do if you make it a priority.

One of us had gotten a blessing right before Gracie was born, saying, "It is important to Heavenly Father that you continue to go to His house. Do not let anything get in the way of that. It is important, at every age, for your children to see you go regularly to the temple. Find babysitters, and He will help provide ways and means to make it happen."

And God did just that. When our first baby was born, we went back to our weekly goal, and it is a perfect strength. It's a wonderful way to refresh and become better as parents and as spouses.

There are plenty of ways to continue to make the temple the centerpiece of your marriage, especially if a temple isn't as accessible. First, make it a priority. Plan a time when you can go, save up money for travel expenses, and get anything you need to make the trip possible, if that is the case. Pick a day to go and plan around it. Stick to it. Spend time reflecting on the promises that we made and the promises that were given to us by God. Respect and wear the temple garment properly. Garments are the Lord's way of letting us take a piece of the temple home with us to have always. They remind us of the way we should live and the promises and strength given to us from Him. During hard times, reflect on the covenants you have made and ponder them—the power in those promises is real. Make the temple important, because it is important.

Just like Joseph Smith taught, we need the temple more than we need anything else. The temple needs to be in the center of our lives and at the core of our marriage. We need to be dedicated to those ordinances and continuously learn and participate more in them. Go prepared and go pondering. But most importantly, go. Go often. Go together. Your lives will be in good order. Escape the real world and feel a little bit of heaven.

The gospel is not our last option; it is our only option. It is truly the only way that we will become and remain happy. The heavens are open, and we have access through the gospel. It is only through our Father in Heaven and His Son, Jesus Christ, that we can overcome, conquer, and receive the greatest blessings to ever exist. When we remember who God truly is, all the power that He has, and that He is for us, it would be foolish not to put Him first. We must not lose sight of why we are truly here and what we need to be doing. We must never forget whose hands we're in. We must never forget that we have a God. We have a God, and He is *ours*. He guides, directs, warns, strengthens, and gives us the greatest things. Choose God every day. Every day, choose eternal salvation. Because when we decide and redecide to choose Heavenly Father, the rest of life seems to fall into place the way it is supposed to. "We know that all things work together for good to them that love God" (Romans 8:28).

LESSON SEVEN

Not Taking Things So Seriously

Bears. Beets. *Battlestar Galactica*.
—Jim Halpert, *The Office*[37]

Ben: Love is quirky. I think you fall in love with someone because of their idiosyncrasies that they may call
imperfections. Initially, you may be drawn to someone because of their looks and who they are, but I
think true love begins when you know their quirks
and their personal characteristics that are peculiar to
them. I know all of my wife's; it's those things that
I love. But one of my favorite *quirks* or *idiosyncrasies*,
or whatever you want to call them, is my wife's ability to burp! Look, Al can win any belching competi-
tion. She may be embarrassed about it, but I think it's
funny. It's the little things like that. Or the face she
doesn't know she makes when she puts on lipstick, or
how loud and animated she is. It's those little quirks
that she has that make Al my wife; I love her for those
things. They are not imperfections; they're the good
stuff. It's the simple things and the silly *quirks* that
make her who she is. And it was those *idiosyncrasies*
that made me fall in love with her.

Life brings plenty of serious things our way without
us having to do anything about it. The real secret to our
marriage? Not taking things so seriously. It's looking for,
and creating, as many opportunities to laugh as we can
every single day, even during the hard times. The secret?
Treating and viewing your spouse less as a business partner,
and every bit as a best friend, because that's what they are:
a best friend on the most wild and amazing adventure that
will last into a completely new world with God.

Marriage is knowing that you are not better than each other. It is holding hands in the grocery store. It's cheering your cups together before you eat. Love is smiling at the *quirks* and looking for the good in each other. Marriage is taking the long way home so you have more time to talk about anything and everything. It's random day trips to try new Mexican restaurants. It's about continually having new inside jokes with one another. Marriage is pausing an episode of *The Office* on Netflix to make out. And it is most definitely about not watching an episode of your show without one another. It's about jumping out from around the corner and scaring the crap out of them because it's funny. Strength comes from doing new things *together.* It comes from holding hands together when you pray every morning and every night and every time in between. It's every bit of the random text messages and the surprise back rubs. The secret to our marriage? It's really no secret at all—it comes from seeking God in all things. Deeper love comes from expressing gratitude for the small things and telling each other really stupid jokes.

Life is better experienced with someone else. Experiences are richer when shared. Trials are easier as a team. Strength is there when you are weak. Humor is perfectly there for the good and the bad. A change of course is more of an adventure when you're not alone. Learning new things from them, and with them, is magic. And the growth you experience over the years is the gem in life.

Because it's life that should be hard, not marriage. It's marriage that should make the hard things in life easier because you have each other and because you have God.

ENDNOTES

1. F. Burton Howard, "Eternal Marriage," *Ensign*, May 2003; italics in original.

2. *Quotes from Coach John Wooden: Winning with Principle* (Nashville: B&H Publishing, 2013), 99.

3. Jeffrey R. Holland, "'Cast Not Away Therefore Your Confidence,'" *Ensign*, March 2000.

4. Gordon B. Hinckley, "'Whosoever Will Save His Life,'" *Ensign*, August 1982.

5. H. Burke Peterson, "Selflessness: A Pattern for Happiness," *Ensign*, May 1985.

6. Thomas S. Monson, "Finding Joy in the Journey," *Ensign*, November 2008.

7. Sylvester Stallone in, "Sly Interview in Parade," *Craig Zablo's StallZone*, accessed June 1, 2017, stallonezone .com/042201parade.html.

8. Thomas S. Monson, "That We May Touch Heaven," *Ensign*, November 1990.

9. Robert L. Simpson, "A Lasting Marriage," *Ensign*, May 1982.

10. Russell M. Nelson, "Nurturing Marriage," *Ensign*, May 2006.

11. Anthony Robbins, *Unlimited Power: The New Science of Personal Achievement* (New York: Simon and Schuster, 2012), 19.

12. Carole M. Stephens in "Elder Holland Talks Candidly About Marriage, Missions, Sexual Sin, and More," *LDSLiving*, accessed May 29, 2017, www.ldsliving .com/Elder-Holland-Talks-Candidly-About-Same-Sex -Attraction-Marriage-Pornography-More/s/81526.

13. Ibid.

14. Lori Cluff Schade, "Marriage, Technology, and Emotional Infidelity," *Ensign*, January 2017.

15. "Improve the Shining Moments," *Hymns*, no. 226.

16. Dieter F. Uchtdorf, "Of Things That Matter Most," *Ensign*, November 2010.

17. Steve Gleason, as quoted in Brad Hicks, "Former Saints Football Player Living Life to the Fullest, Despite Diagnosis with ALS," *Fox 6 Now*, posted November 14, 2012, www.fox6now.com/2012/11/14 /former-saints-football-player-living-life-to-the-fullest -despite-diagnosis-with-als/.

18. "Discover Your Love Language," *The 5 Love Languages*, accessed May 31, 2017, www.5lovelanguages.com /profile/.

19. Elizabeth Gilbert, *Eat, Pray, Love: One Woman's Search for Everything Across Italy, India and Indonesia* (New York: Riverhead Books, 2006), 298.

20. "Falling Out of Love with a Spouse," 4:42, *Mormon Channel*, www.mormonchannel.org/watch/series/his -grace/falling-out-of-love-with-a-spouse.

21. Ibid.

22. Ibid.

23. Ibid.

24. Ibid.

25. Richard G. Scott, "The Eternal Blessings of Marriage," *Ensign*, May 2011.

26. *Teachings of the Prophet Joseph Smith*, sel. Joseph Fielding Smith (1976), 256.

27. Jeffrey R. Holland's recorded address DVD, included in Jeffrey R. Holland, *For Times of Trouble: Spiritual Solace from the Psalms* (Salt Lake City: Deseret Book, 2012).

28. John Wooden and Jay Carty, *Coach Wooden One-On-One: Inspiring Conversations on Purpose, Passion and the Pursuit of Success* (Grand Rapids, MI: Baker Publishing, 2003).

29. Dieter F. Uchtdorf, "Living the Gospel Joyful," *Ensign*, November 2014.

30. Ibid.

31. Jeffrey R. Holland in, "Wrong Roads," *LDS Media Library*, 3:58, www.lds.org/media-library/video/2013 -09-016-wrong-roads.

32. Andrew Hill and John Wooden, *Be Quick—But Don't Hurry!: Finding Success in the Teachings of a Lifetime* (New York: Simon & Schuster, 2001), 117.

33. Spencer W. Kimball, "Small Acts of Service," *Ensign*, December 1974.

34. Marjorie Pay Hinckley in, Elyssa Andrus and Marc Haddock, "Marjorie Hinckley, 1911–2004," *Daily Herald*, April 7, 2004.

35. Ezra Taft Benson, "The Great Commandment—Love the Lord," *Ensign*, May 1988.

36. Sheri Dew, "You Were Born to Lead, You Were Born for Glory," *BYU Speeches*, December 9, 2003, speeches.byu.edu/talks/sheri-l-dew_born-lead-born -glory/#byu-ribbon.

37. Brent Forrester and Justin Spitzer, "Product Recall," *The Office*, season 3, episode 20, directed by Randall Einhorn, aired April 26, 2007 (Universal City, CA: Universal Studios Home Entertainment, 2007), DVD.

ABOUT THE AUTHOR

Al Carraway

Al Carraway is a multi-award-winning LDS speaker and blogger and is the author of the best-selling book *More Than the Tattooed Mormon*.

Al was born and raised in Rochester, New York, where she earned her degree in graphic design and marketing. She became a member of The Church of Jesus Christ of Latter-day Saints in 2009 and has since written about her relationship with God, her experiences, lessons, and trials on www.alcarraway.com. Since 2010, she has found herself traveling across the country every week speaking to LDS audiences of all kinds—those at youth camps, firesides, and even prisons. Al shares her conversion story and teaches all those who will listen how to keep going in hard times and of the reality of God and this Church. Her passion it is to tell everyone that happiness exists and that it comes from this gospel. She is a lover of the outdoors and waking up early. She is a taco enthusiast, a journal addict, and is happiest when she is with her husband, Ben, and their two kids, Gracie and Christian.

ABOUT THE AUTHOR

Ben Carraway

Benjamin (Ben) A. Carraway was born in Nürnberg, Germany, and raised in West Valley City, Utah. Ben graduated from Arizona State University with a degree in organizational leadership and is pursuing his graduate degree in leadership studies and higher education administration. He has a passion for becoming better and helping others do the same. Ben created a personal growth website and blog titled *High Thrive* that is centered on helping others discover their potential and become better. Ben is married to his sweetheart, Al, and is the father of Gracie and Christian.

Scan to visit

www.alcarraway.com